GAMING

FROM ATARI TO XBOX

COMPUTING AND CONNECTING IN THE 21ST CENTURY

GAMING

FROM ATARI TO XBOX

EDITED BY MICHAEL RAY, ASSISTANT EDITOR, GEOGRAPHY AND POPULAR CULTURE

Britannica®
Educational Publishing

IN ASSOCIATION WITH

ROSEN
EDUCATIONAL SERVICES

Published in 2012 by Britannica Educational Publishing
(a trademark of Encyclopædia Britannica, Inc.)
in association with Rosen Educational Services, LLC
29 East 21st Street, New York, NY 10010.

Distributed exclusively by Rosen Educational Services.
For a listing of additional Britannica Educational Publishing titles, call toll free (800) 237-9932.

First Edition

Britannica Educational Publishing
Michael I. Levy: Executive Editor
J.E. Luebering: Senior Manager
Adam Augustyn: Assistant Manager, Encyclopædia Britannica
Marilyn L. Barton: Senior Coordinator, Production Control
Steven Bosco: Director, Editorial Technologies
Lisa S. Braucher: Senior Producer and Data Editor
Yvette Charboneau: Senior Copy Editor
Kathy Nakamura: Manager, Media Acquisition
Michael Ray: Assistant Editor, Geography and Popular Culture

Rosen Educational Services
Jeanne Nagle: Senior Editor
Nelson Sá: Art Director
Cindy Reiman: Photography Manager
Amy Feinberg: Photo Researcher
Brian Garvey: Designer, Cover Design
Introduction by Michael Ray

Library of Congress Cataloging-in-Publication Data

Gaming: from Atari to Xbox/edited by Michael Ray.
     p. cm.—(Computing and connecting in the 21st century)
In association with Britannica Educational Publishing, Rosen Educational Services.
Includes bibliographical references and index.
ISBN 978-1-61530-704-3 (library binding)
1. Video games. 2. Computer games. I. Ray, Michael.
GV1469.3.G427 2012
794.8—dc23

                                                                      2011035886

Manufactured in the United States of America

CONTENTS

83

88

98

INTRODUCTION

In little more than half a century, electronic games have evolved from novel curiosities created by university computer science departments to a multi-billion-dollar global entertainment phenomenon. Iconic game characters such as Pac-Man, Mario, and Lara Croft have achieved a level of name recognition on par with celebrities and historical figures. Successful games can generate more revenue in a single day than a major Hollywood movie can during its entire box office run—and several games have themselves been made into movies.

This evolution did not happen in a vacuum, however. The popularity of electronic games has ebbed and flowed for a number of reasons. Players have shifted from the arcade to home consoles, from personal computers to handheld devices, as technological advances or "killer apps" (games that are desirable enough to inspire a player to purchase an entirely new gaming system) have made different platforms more appealing. Improved graphics and portability differentiate the latest generation of consoles from their predecessors, but the ability to compete or cooperate with other human players over a network has restored a social element to electronic gaming that recalls the earliest video arcades.

There has also been a divergence in the perceived target audience of electronic games. Traditionally, "video games" had been dismissed as a plaything of young boys. Over time, it became apparent that men and women of every age were enjoying electronic games, and the market responded accordingly. Family friendly fare, such as the party games commonly found on the Nintendo Wii, appealed to a broad demographic; the widespread success of that system indicated that the Wii's programmers had hit their mark. Conversely, games specifically targeting a mature audience, such as the *Grand Theft Auto* franchise, posted strong sales with stories that featured sexual situations, violence, and emotionally complex characters who would not have been out of place in a well-written R-rated film.

The creation of such a diverse catalog of games could not have been foreseen when William Higinbotham created *Tennis for Two* in 1958. Intended as a technology demonstration for visitors to Brookhaven National Laboratory in New York, the game was played on an analog computer, using an oscilloscope as a screen. *Tennis for Two* featured simple controls—a rotating dial varied the angle of the player's "racquet," and a single button dictated the timing of serves and volleys. The game was an immediate hit, as spectators gathered around the five-inch display to watch as a glowing dot (representing the ball) bounced back and forth across the simulated tennis court. The following year, programmers replaced the small display with a larger screen and added gameplay options that allowed players to simulate tennis in a low-gravity environment (such as the Moon) or a high-gravity environment (such as Jupiter).

A few years later and a short distance away, a group of young programmers at Massachusetts Institute of

Technology were exploring the capabilities of Digital Equipment Corporation's new Programmed Data Processor (PDP) minicomputer. DEC had donated a PDP-1 to MIT, and students were eager to demonstrate what the machine could do. Weighing more than half a ton, measuring 8 feet (2.4 metres) tall and 6 feet (1.8 metres) wide, and outfitted with a 16-inch CRT display and Soroban typewriter that had been modified to act as an input/output device, the PDP-1 was the state of the art in laboratory computing. With a price tag of $120,000, programmers frequently added the prefix "Expensive" to describe PDP-1 program functions; for example, Expensive Typewriter replicated the function of a standard electric typewriter at roughly a thousand times the cost. Expensive Planetarium was a slowly scrolling star map created by MIT student Peter Samson.

The latter would serve as a key element in the next great step in electronic gaming: a space combat simulator called *Spacewar!* Created by Steve Russell and others at MIT in 1962, *Spacewar!* offered players the straightforward and satisfying goal of blowing up one another's space ships with torpedoes. Complicating matters was a central star that exerted a gravitational pull on both ships and the torpedoes that they fired. Expensive Planetarium served as the background to the battle, providing a series of visual reference points that allowed players to better gauge the speed and direction of the ships. As both a technology demonstration and an addictive time-killer, *Spacewar!* was a massive success. Russell freely shared the game's programming code, and by the mid-1960s, *Spacewar!* could be found on virtually every minicomputer capable of running it.

Of course, it was only a matter of time before someone realized that there was money to be made in electronic games. By the early 1970s, computers had become smaller, cheaper, and more powerful. Transistors gave way to microprocessors, and the computing power of the PDP-1 could now be contained in a housing that was a fraction of the original's size.

It was in this climate that a man named Nolan Bushnell sought to create the first successful coin-operated electronic game. In 1971 Bushnell and colleague Ted Dabney designed a standalone coin-operated version of *Spacewar!* that they called *Computer Space*. Although *Computer Space* was a failure, the design of its cabinet would influence coin-operated arcade games for generations to come. Bushnell and Dabney would find greater success with their second effort—a table tennis simulator called *Pong*. Bushnell, Dabney, and engineer Al Alcorn founded the Atari Corporation in 1972, and they released *Pong* under the Atari banner later that year.

In 1974, after producing thousands of coin-operated *Pong* machines, Atari found itself facing a lawsuit from the pioneers in the field of home electronic gaming, Sanders Associates and Magnavox. In 1966, Ralph Baer, a manager at Sanders Associates, devised a simple game involving player-controlled dots that chased each other across a television screen. Intrigued, Sanders management authorized Baer to further explore the television game concept. Baer's team experimented with both game ideas and delivery mechanisms (initial plans suggested that cable television could be used to supplement gaming content). By 1968 Baer and his "TV Game Project" team had produced the Brown Box—so named for the simulated wood paneling that covered its exterior—a prototype home gaming console that played 12 different games, including table tennis.

As Sanders was primarily a defense contractor, marketing a home video game system was far outside its realm of expertise. Baer's team approached a number of different parties over the following years; Baer and Sanders submitted a patent application for a "television gaming and training apparatus" in 1971. Later that year, Sanders reached an exclusive licensing agreement with television manufacturer Magnavox, and in 1972 Magnavox debuted the commercial version of the Brown Box, dubbed the Odyssey home video game console.

Magnavox sponsored a series of promotional technology demonstrations across the United States to herald the Odyssey's release. One of the attendees at the Silicon Valley event was Nolan Bushnell. Although he later claimed that he developed the idea for *Pong* prior to his exposure to the Odyssey table tennis game, Bushnell's troubles with Sanders and Magnavox were more profound than the questionable origin of Atari's flagship game. With the granting of U.S. patent 3,728,480 on April 17, 1973, Sanders and Magnavox were essentially the gatekeepers for future home video game development.

Over the next decade, virtually every video game developer would find itself facing a legal challenge from Sanders and Magnavox. Bushnell and Atari settled with Magnavox in 1974, becoming the first sublicensees under the "480" patent. A courtroom victory over manufacturers Seeburg and Bally-Midway demonstrated the strength of Magnavox's legal position. Other patents, most notably RE28,507 (granted to Sanders employee William Rusch in 1975), further improved the legal standing of Sanders and Magnavox. While it might seem that such a dominant position in the young but growing market of electronic games must have been achieved through patent filings that were extremely broad, the reverse was the case. Baer's original "480" patent was actually quite specific, and it spelled out exactly how the console unit would interact with a television display and how players would manipulate specific onscreen elements. It was this specificity that fueled an uninterrupted string of courtroom victories for Sanders and Magnavox: against Mattel, makers of the Intellivision console; against Activision, the first third-party developer of electronic games; and against Nintendo, who tried unsuccessfully to challenge the Baer patent on the basis that Higinbotham's *Tennis for Two* was the first true electronic game (a claim that was rejected in 1989).

These early legal escapades did little to stifle the growth of the industry, however. Atari's first home console, later dubbed the Atari 2600, sold tens of millions of units worldwide. In fact, the home console gamer was soon awash with options. Atari boasted a wide selection of titles adapted from the most popular arcade games, while Mattel's Intellivision replaced the traditional joystick with a unique disc-shaped controller and offered games that incorporated simulated human voices. Coleco's ColecoVision system boasted greatly improved graphics and a wide assortment of peripherals. Third-party developers such as Activision and Imagic, each founded by former Atari programmers, pushed the limits of existing game technology with fantastic visuals and addictive game play.

And then the market collapsed. For every one Activision, there were dozens of companies offering games that were, at best, of middling quality. A "wild west" atmosphere had seized the industry, with unlikely companies such as breakfast food manufacturer Quaker

Oats entering the market to capitalize on the electronic game craze. The console market became flooded with cheap, poor-quality titles; consumers rejected electronic gaming on a wholesale level, with diehards turning their attention to the emerging home computer market.

Although the Apple II and the IBM Personal Computer were both robust gaming platforms, their price tags—which ranged from $1,500 to $2,500—placed them far outside the budgets of casual gamers. With the console market in freefall, microcomputer manufacturer Commodore introduced the Commodore 64, a home computer that featured color graphics, an impressive (at the time) 64KB of RAM, and a price tag that quickly settled around the $200 mark. Commodore sold some 20 million C64s, and some of the best games of the 1980s found their widest exposure on that system. Sid Meier's *Pirates*, Richard Garriott's *Ultima* franchise, the "Gold Box" *Advanced Dungeons & Dragons* titles from Strategic Simulations, Inc., Lucasfilm's earliest adventure games, and the outstanding *Summer/Winter/California Games* series from Epyx were notable C64 games.

In addition to the host of productivity applications that set them apart from consoles, computers also featured numerous enhancements that changed the way games were played. The keyboard allowed for more robust control configurations than a standard console joystick, an improvement that was readily apparent in such games as flight simulators and military strategy titles. Perhaps more profound, though, was the integration of internal hard drives, or floppy disk drives, which gave users the ability to save their progress in a given game, with the intention of returning to it later. This feature would be a crucial element in the next generation of console games, as Miyamoto Shigeru—a man who would come to be known as "the Steven Spielberg of electronic games"—prepared to make his mark on the industry with a Japanese company named Nintendo.

Miyamoto was not yet 30 years old when he created *Donkey Kong*, a seminal platform game featuring a barrel-throwing ape and an intrepid plumber who would eventually come to be known as Mario. A massive hit at arcades (and the inspiration for a flurry of sequels), *Donkey Kong* was a popular console title prior to the 1983 market implosion. Nintendo sought to fill the subsequent void with the Nintendo Entertainment System (NES), an eight-bit console that debuted in the United States in February 1986. Already a success in Japan, the NES shipped with a selection of titles that included *Super Mario Bros.*, Miyamoto's second franchise-launching game and the killer app that drove the rebirth of the home console market. Miyamoto's *The Legend of Zelda* soon followed, and its battery backup feature—an innovation that granted console players the "save game" feature long enjoyed by computer gamers—combined with a breakthrough inventory management system and a complex, engaging story made it one of the landmark titles in the history of electronic games.

The *Donkey Kong*, *Mario*, and *Zelda* franchises would ultimately generate dozens of titles, collectively selling more than 350 million games worldwide. Their popular and critical success would assure Miyamoto a place in the ranks of electronic gaming royalty. His ongoing list of innovations (which included Nintendo's Wii system and the *Wii Fit* game) meant that Miyamoto, perhaps more than any other individual, had personally lifted electronic games from the doldrums of the early '80s and ensured their survival and popularity into the 21st century.

CHAPTER 1

DEFINITION OF ELECTRONIC GAMING

Electronic games, also called computer games or video games, are interactive games operated by computer circuitry. The machines, or "platforms," on which electronic games are played include general-purpose shared and personal computers, arcade consoles, video consoles connected to home television sets, handheld game machines, mobile devices such as cellular phones, and server-based networks. The term *video game* can be used to represent the totality of these formats, but often it refers more specifically to games played on devices with video displays, such as televisions and arcade consoles.

FROM CHESS TO *SPACEWAR!* TO *PONG*

The idea of playing games on computers is almost as old as the computer itself. Initially, the payoffs expected from this activity were closely related to the study of computation. For example, the mathematician and engineer Claude Shannon proposed in 1950 that computers could be programmed to play chess, and he questioned whether this would mean that a computer could think. Shannon's proposal stimulated decades of research on chess- and checkers-playing programs, generally by computer scientists working in the field of artificial intelligence.

Many computer games grew out of university and industrial computer laboratories, often as technology demonstrations or "after hours" amusements of computer programmers and engineers. For example, in 1958 William A. Higinbotham of the Brookhaven National Laboratory in New York used an analog computer, control boxes, and an oscilloscope to create *Tennis for Two* as part of a public display for visitors to the laboratory. Only a few years later, Steve Russell, Alan Kotok, J. Martin Graetz, and others created *Spacewar!* (1962) at the Massachusetts Institute of Technology (MIT). This game began as a demonstration program to show off the PDP-1 minicomputer donated by Digital Equipment Corporation (DEC) to MIT and the new Precision CRT Display Type 30 attached to it. This new technology appealed to the "hacker" culture of the Tech Model Railroad Club on campus, and its authors were members of this group. They wrote software and built control boxes that gave players the ability to move spaceships depicted on accurate star maps, maneuvering about and firing space torpedoes in a competitive match.

With the widespread adoption of PDPs on other campuses and laboratories in the 1960s and '70s, *Spacewar!* was soon ubiquitous. One such institution was the University of Utah, home of a strong program in computer graphics and an electrical engineering student named Nolan

William A. Hinginbotham's Tennis for Two *display at Brookhaven National Laboratory.* Courtesy of Brookhaven National Laboratory

Bushnell. After graduating, Bushnell moved to Silicon Valley to work for the Ampex Corporation. Bushnell had worked at an amusement park during college, and, after playing *Spacewar!*, he dreamed of filling entertainment arcades with such computer games. Together with one of his coworkers at Ampex, Ted Dabney, Bushnell designed *Computer Space* (1971), a coin-operated version of *Spacewar!* set in a wildly futuristic arcade cabinet. Although the game—manufactured and marketed by Nutting Associates, a vendor of coin-operated arcades—was a commercial failure, it established a design and general technical configuration for arcade consoles.

In 1972 Bushnell, Dabney, and Al Alcorn, another Ampex alumnus, founded the Atari Corporation. Bushnell asked Alcorn to design a simple game based on Ping-Pong, explaining by way of inspiration that Atari had received a contract to make it. While there was in fact no such contract, Alcorn was adept at television electronics and produced a simple and addictive game, which they named *Pong*. Unable to interest manufacturers of pinball games in this prototype, Bushnell and Alcorn installed it in a local bar, where it became an immediate success as a coin-operated game. After clearing a legal obstacle posed by the Magnavox Company's hold on the patent for video games, Atari geared up to manufacture arcade consoles in volume. It thus created the "coin-op" game industry, achieving such success that it drew competitors into its new business space, the electronic game arcade, which became perhaps the main source for innovative electronic games well into the 1980s.

EARLY HOME VIDEO CONSOLES

After computers and arcades, the third inspiration for early electronic games was television. Ralph Baer, a television engineer and manager at the military electronics firm of Sanders Associates (later integrated into BAE Systems), began in the late 1960s to develop technology and design games that could be played on television sets. In 1966 Baer designed circuitry to display and control moving dots on a television screen, leading to a simple chase game that he called *Fox and Hounds*. With this success in hand, Baer secured permission and funding from Sanders management to assemble a small group, the TV Game Project. Within a year several promising game designs had been demonstrated, and Baer's group experimented with ways of delivering games to households by means such as cable television. In 1968 they completed the Brown Box, a solid-state prototype for a video game console. Three years later Baer was granted a U.S. patent for a "television gaming apparatus." Magnavox acquired the rights soon thereafter, leading in 1972 to production of the first home video console, the Magnavox Odyssey.

The success of *Pong* as a coin-operated game led a number of companies, including Atari itself, to forge ahead with home versions and imitations of the game. Seeking to expand its coin-operated arcade business, Atari reached agreement with Sears, Roebuck and Company to manufacture and distribute the home version of *Pong*. Its success intensified the already brutal competition in this market. The Fairchild Channel F, released in 1976, and the Atari 2600 VCS (Video Computer System), released in 1977, led a new generation of consoles that used programmable ROM cartridges for distribution and storage of game software. These systems were programmable in the sense that different game cartridges could be inserted into special slots—a technical step that encouraged the separation of game development from hardware design.

ATARI CONSOLE

The Atari video game console was released in 1977 by the North American game manufacturer Atari, Inc. Using a cartridge-based system that allowed users to play a variety of video games, the Atari console marked the beginning of a new era in home gaming systems.

Developed by Atari cofounder Nolan Bushnell and a team of designers, the console connected to a standard television set and employed computer chips that featured full-colour graphics and sound. The system, originally called the Atari VCS (Video Computer System), came bundled with two joysticks, two paddle controllers, and one game cartridge. Nine games were initially offered for it. The system was also sold at Sears department stores under the name Sears Video Arcade.

Success was assured in 1980 after Atari released a home version of the Japanese video game *Space Invaders*. Sales doubled as millions purchased the console to play the popular arcade game at home. The original console was renamed Atari 2600 following the release of the more advanced Atari 5200, and a variety of other titles were developed for it, including *Adventure*, *Asteroids*, *Breakout*, *Demon Attack*, *Frogger*, *Pac-Man*, and *Pong*.

With sales of more than 30 million over a span of three decades, the Atari 2600 became one of the most popular gaming systems in history. Although production of the console halted in the early 1990s, the system still enjoys popularity among classic game aficionados, who continue to develop new games for it. In 2004 Atari released the Atari Flashback 2, which contains 40 classic games and mimics the look of the original Atari 2600, including the iconic joystick, for play on newer console systems and personal computers (PCs). Atari continues to make games for PCs and all the major consoles.

Activision, founded in 1979 by four former Atari game designers, was the first company exclusively focused on game software. By 1983, however, a flood of poorly designed game titles for the leading home consoles led to a consumer backlash and a sharp decline in the video console industry, shifting momentum back to computer-based games.

ACTIVISION INC.

Activision was founded in 1979 by David Crane and Alan Miller—game designers who split with Atari over issues of creator's rights—and entertainment executive Jim Levy. Their response was to create a company where designers would be an essential part of the brand identity, with the lead developer of a given title receiving credit on the game box. Soon after the company's formation, they were joined by fellow Atari designers Larry Kaplan and Bob Whitehead. As the electronic gaming industry's first third-party software developer, Activision immediately faced a legal challenge from Atari, which attempted to preserve its monopoly on games for the Atari VCS system. That suit was settled in 1982, but by that time Activision had already established itself as a thriving competitor in an expanding industry. Games such as *Chopper Command* and *River Raid* sported vibrant graphics and fluid gameplay, and *Pitfall!* represented one of the earliest examples of the platform game genre.

The success of Activision inspired a wave of imitators, and soon the market was flooded with games of dubious quality. Between 1983 and 1984 the industry collapsed under the weight of its own overexpansion. Activision weathered the storm by shifting its focus to the burgeoning home computer market, but the ill-timed acquisition of text-based adventure game publisher Infocom almost doomed the company. A corporate reorganization led to the departure of much of the company's creative talent, including the last of its founders, and in 1988 the Activision name was abandoned in favour of Mediagenic, as executives attempted to rebrand the company as a multipurpose software developer. Mediagenic struggled to stay afloat, but a change in ownership and management in 1990 signaled a dramatic turnaround. The company renamed itself Activision in 1992, and it spent the next few years building on the successes of its past, releasing titles such as *Return to Zork* (1993), a graphic adventure based on a classic Infocom game, and *Pitfall: The Mayan Adventure* (1994), an addictive platform game.

Activision acquired a new generation of talented designers, and it won critical acclaim with PC offerings like *Interstate '76* (1997), a stylish, funk-infused, 3D vehicle combat game that anticipated such later titles as *Grand Theft Auto* from Rockstar Games. The company also forged lucrative partnerships with independent developers. Although development costs for new games soared, with a typical game costing millions of dollars to bring to market, Activision continued to post profits through the late 1990s and early 2000s.

INTERACTIVE FICTION

Games developed for the first arcade and home consoles emphasized simplicity and action. This was partly out of necessity, due to the limitations of rudimentary display technologies, microprocessors, and other components and to the limited memory available for programs. (These traits also reflected the goal of creating arcade games that would quickly swallow as many coins as possible.) Still, while the designs of games such as Atari's *Breakout* (1976) or Taito's *Space Invaders* (1978) were elegantly streamlined, these arcade hits generally offered little in terms of strategic depth, narrative, or simulation value. By the mid-1970s, however, several computer games challenged these restrictions. These games relied on text, networking, or other capabilities available on computers in academic laboratories.

One of the first was *Hunt the Wumpus*, which appeared in several versions for different systems. Kenneth Thompson, a researcher at Bell Laboratories, wrote one version in C for the UNIX operating system, which he had codeveloped; Gregory Yob wrote another in BASIC that was distributed widely through listings in early computer game magazines. Both versions were probably written in 1972. *Hunt the Wumpus* and games like it introduced the notion of defining a virtual space. Players explored this space by inputting simple text commands—such as room numbers or coordinates—from their keyboards. They enjoyed considerable freedom of navigation in exploring the caves, dungeons, and castles that were typical of such text-based games. Moreover, computer software could be easily shared, modified, and extended by programmers, resulting in a great variety of similar games.

The defining computer game of the 1970s was Will Crowther's *Colossal Cave Adventure*, probably completed in 1977. Text-based games of its ilk have since been known commonly as "adventure games." Crowther combined his experiences exploring Kentucky's Mammoth and Flint Ridge caves and playing *Dungeons & Dragons*-style role-playing games with fantasy themes reminiscent of J.R.R. Tolkien's *Lord of the Rings*. Written in the programming language FORTRAN for the PDP-10 computer, *Adventure* became the prototype for an entirely new category of games, usually called "interactive fiction," that boasted a new narrative structure. Such games shaped the player's experience with descriptions of rooms, characters, and items and a story that evolved in response to the player's choices. In *Adventure* this meant wandering through a dungeon to collect items and defeat monsters, but later titles featured more elaborate narratives. In 1977 Don Woods of the Stanford Artificial Intelligence Laboratory came across a copy of the source code for *Adventure* and carefully revised the game, adding new elements that increased its popularity. This version and its variants were widely distributed by users of DEC minicomputers. By the late 1970s, home computers and video game consoles had also made commercial distribution of these games possible, and text-based or simple graphical versions of *Adventure* were provided for many of these systems.

PERSONAL COMPUTER GAMES

By the late 1970s, electronic games could be designed not only for large, university-based shared computers, video consoles, and arcade machines but also for

Zork

Will Crowther's *Adventure* was the prototype for text-based computer games organized as interactive stories. But in 1977 several students at the Massachusetts Institute of Technology (MIT) decided that they could write more sophisticated interactive fiction by abandoning FORTRAN, the programming language used for *Adventure*, in favour of MDL, which was a descendant of LISP, a language that grew out of research in artificial intelligence. The characteristics of MDL enabled the students to build a database of objects in their game that greatly simplified the construction of rooms and game items—of which there were roughly 400 in all. The game was given the nonsense name *Zork*.

Practically any computer science student at a major American university could play the game by logging in to MIT over ARPANET (the precursor to the Internet), and *Zork* quickly gained cult status. In 1979 *Zork*'s programmers decided to form their own company, Infocom, and create a version of the game for personal computers. Soon *Zork* was available for every popular brand of PC. Infocom became the leading publisher of adventure games during the 1980s and was closely identified with interactive fiction as a genre.

the new breed of home computers equipped with their own general-purpose microprocessors. Apple II (1977) from Apple Computer, Inc. (now Apple Inc.), and the IBM Personal Computer (1981) featured colour graphics, flexible storage capacity, and a variety of input devices. The Atari 800 (1979) and Commodore Business Machines' Commodore 64 (1982) offered similar features, but they also retained cartridge slots for console-style games.

Game designers took advantage of the greater flexibility of computers to explore new game genres, often inspired by complex paper-and-pencil role-playing games such as *Dungeons & Dragons*, various board games, and Crowther's *Adventure*. Interactive fiction was a particularly successful format on personal computers. Infocom, perhaps the most successful computer game company of the early 1980s, adapted this style of game to a variety of literary formats, such as science fiction and mysteries. Infocom began with the popular *Zork* series, inspired directly by *Adventure*. Infocom games disdained graphics, relying on methods that allowed for more varied player input and story building and incorporating techniques such as language parsing and database programming learned by its founders at MIT to stimulate the player's imagination.

Other games—such as the *King's Quest* series by Sierra On-Line (1983), military simulations and role-playing games published by Strategic Simulations Incorporated (founded in 1979), Richard Garriott's *Akalabeth/Ultima* series (1979), and the sports and multimedia titles of Electronic Arts (founded in 1982)—extended the simulation and storytelling capacity of computer games. Networked games added a social dimension. *Empire* had been developed as part of the PLATO (Programmed Logic for Automatic Teaching Operations) Project at the University of Illinois during the early 1970s, and the possibilities of social interaction and networked-based graphics were thoroughly explored as part of this project and the games that resulted from it. *MUD* (Multi User Dungeon), developed in 1979 by Roy Trubshaw and Richard Bartle at the University of Essex, England, combined interactive fiction, role-playing, programming, and dial-up modem access to a shared computer. It inspired dozens of popular multiplayer games, known collectively as MUDs, that placed players in a virtual world that functioned on the basis of social interaction as much as structured game play. Hundreds of themed multiplayer MUDs were written during the 1980s and early '90s.

THE RETURN OF VIDEO CONSOLES

Two Japanese manufacturers of coin-operated video games, the Nintendo Co., Ltd., and Sega Enterprises Ltd., introduced a new generation of video consoles, the Nintendo Entertainment System (NES; 1985) and the Sega Genesis (1989), with graphics that equaled or exceeded the capabilities of personal computers. More important, Nintendo introduced battery-powered storage cartridges that enabled players to save games in progress. Games such as Nintendo's *Super Mario Bros.* (1985) and *The Legend of Zelda* (1987), as well as Squaresoft's *Final Fantasy* series (1987; originally for Nintendo only), fully exploited the ability to save games in progress; they used it to provide deeper game experiences, flexible character development, and complex interactive environments. These qualities encouraged comparisons between video games and other narrative media such as cinema.

SEGA CORPORATION

Sega Corporation is a software and hardware company created in the United States but is now based in Japan. Sega originated in 1940 as Standard Games, a coin-operated game company in Hawaii.

While providing games for military bases, the company was called Standard Games, but, following a move to Japan in 1952, the company was renamed Service Games of Japan. Service Games of Japan later merged with Rosen Enterprises to create Sega Enterprises. Sega released a popular arcade game called *Periscope* in 1965 and also created arcade standouts *Zaxxon* (1982) and *Out Run* (1986). In the early 1980s, Sega released its first console system, the SG-1000, which generated more than $200 million in revenue. Over the next few years, Sega underwent several ownership changes. The company released more consoles—the Sega Master System (1986) and the Sega Genesis (1988)—beginning a serious competition with its main rival, the Nintendo console, for control of the video game market.

After seeing the Master System defeated by the Nintendo Entertainment System (NES), Sega launched an aggressive marketing campaign and, with the help of the Sega Genesis's superior technology, was able to recapture a large portion of the video game market. When the Super Nintendo Entertainment System (SNES) was released in the early 1990s, Sega introduced *Sonic the Hedgehog*, a platform game whose speedy blue namesake soon became the face of the company. Sonic was designed to seem more modern than Nintendo's mascot, Mario, from the *Mario Bros.* game series, and he went on to appear in many popular games. A long battle for video supremacy with Nintendo ensued, which resulted in Sega's defeat; nevertheless, both companies thrived throughout the so-called console wars.

Sega went on to create several more console systems, including the Saturn in 1994 and the Dreamcast in 1998, but new companies entering the competition and poor sales caused Sega to abandon console development entirely in 2001. Sega has since focused on software design and worked as a third-party game developer for its most successful franchises, such as *Sonic the Hedgehog* and *Virtua Fighter*.

In 1989 Nintendo extended its business success with the introduction of Game Boy, a handheld game system with a small monochrome display. It was not the first portable game player—Nintendo had marketed the small Game and Watch player since 1980—but it offered a new puzzle game, Alexey Pajitnov's *Tetris* (1989), an international best-seller that was ideally suited to the new device. More units of Game Boy, continued by the Game Boy Advance in 2001, have been sold than any other game device.

A game player operates an early Nintendo Game Boy handheld system.
Valerie Quentin/Gamma-Rapho via Getty Images

NOTABLE EARLY ELECTRONIC GAMES

Although they might appear graphically primitive to players accustomed to the lifelike visuals displayed on next-generation consoles and PCs, these early titles had a profound influence on later games.

Pong

Pong, a groundbreaking electronic game, was released in 1972 by the American game manufacturer Atari, Inc. One of the earliest video games, *Pong* became wildly popular and helped launch the video game industry. The original *Pong* consisted of two paddles that players used to volley a small ball back and forth across a screen.

The German-born American television engineer Ralph Baer laid the groundwork for *Pong* in 1958 when he proposed making simple video games that people could play on their home television sets. The Magnavox Odyssey, known as the first console video game system, was released in 1972 and offered an electronic game of table tennis, or Ping-Pong. Atari founder Nolan Bushnell created *Pong*, his version of this concept, as an arcade game. A small company at the time, Atari began manufacturing the games in an old roller-skating rink, and by 1972 the company had sold more than 8,000 *Pong* arcade machines. In 1975 Atari turned *Pong* into a console system game. After striking an exclusive deal with Sears, Roebuck and Company, *Pong* was soon in the homes of many American families. *Pong*'s popularity declined in the 1980s as video games temporarily went out of style, but it had already secured its place in history as the most popular arcade game up to that time.

In 1974 the makers of the Magnavox Odyssey sued Atari for stealing the concept for *Pong*. Magnavox won the lawsuit in 1977, upholding the company's patent, but by then Atari had already licensed the patent for $700,000.

Pac-Man

In 1980 the Japanese arcade game manufacturer Namco Limited introduced the world to *Pac-Man*. The lead designer was Iwatani Tohru, who intended to create a game that did not emphasize violence. By paying careful attention to themes, design, and colours, Iwatani hoped that Namco could market an arcade game that would appeal to females. The game concept was therefore inspired by food and eating, as opposed to the shooting of space aliens and other foes that prevailed in most arcade games of the time. Instead, players maneuvered through a simple maze with a joystick, devouring coloured dots until all were gone, thereby completing a level and moving on to the next maze. In Japanese slang, *paku paku* describes the snapping of a mouth open and shut, and thus the central character, resembling a small pizza with a slice cut out for the mouth, was given the name Pac-Man. The game was made challenging by a group of four "ghosts" on each level that tried to catch and consume Pac-Man; the roles of predator and prey were temporarily reversed when Pac-Man ate special "power pills" placed in the maze.

Pac-Man quickly became an international sensation, with more than 100,000 consoles sold in the United States alone, easily making it the most successful arcade game in history. When players learned that the ghosts moved in patterns, they became obsessed with devising precise routes for Pac-Man to follow. Yet this apparent predictability was offset by the sheer number of levels

(256), which added immense complexity to the quest for the perfect game. (In 1999 a Florida resident finally earned this distinction by scoring 3,333,360 points during a six-hour session.)

With its innovative design, *Pac-Man* had a greater impact on popular culture than any other video game. Guides to playing *Pac-Man* emerged on best-seller lists in the United States, soon followed by popular songs, a cartoon television series, merchandise, and magazine articles, as well as countless versions and imitations of the game for every electronic gaming platform.

Tetris

Created by Russian designer Alexey Pajitnov in 1985, *Tetris* allows players to rotate falling blocks strategically to clear levels. Pajitnov claimed he created the name of the game by combining the Greek prefix *tetra*, which refers to the four squares contained in each block, with the word *tennis*.

Tetris has been released for virtually every computer and electronic gaming system, and it is often revered as a classic. Though numerous sequels have been spawned, *Tetris* games almost always have the same play mechanics: differently shaped blocks drop at varying speeds, and, as the blocks descend, the player must rotate and arrange them to create an uninterrupted horizontal row on the screen. When the player forms one or more solid rows, the completed rows disappear. The goal of the game is to prevent the blocks from stacking up to the top of the screen for as long as possible. Subsequent versions of the game included different modes of play and unique twists, but the overall game play usually mirrored the original *Tetris* quite closely.

The *Tetris* franchise endured years of litigation regarding licensing rights, but this did not stop the game from being featured on Nintendo's Game Boy, where it rose to stardom. Later versions, however, incited anger among *Tetris* purists, who objected to an "infinite spin" mechanic that afforded the player additional time to place a block by rotating the block rapidly as it descended.

The Legend of Zelda

When Nintendo released *The Legend of Zelda* for the Japanese market in 1986, it marked a new era in the culture, technology, and business of video games. The game's designer, Miyamoto Shigeru, was already a star, having produced *Donkey Kong* and the *Mario Bros.* series. Now he wanted to push further the concept of open-ended game

Oh, thank you so much!

Princess Zelda thanks her rescuer in a still from the electronic game Legend of Zelda: Twilight Princess, released in 2005. Mike Fanous/

play by giving players a large but unified world in which they could discover their own path for the development of the main character, named Link. Miyamoto's design exploited the improvements in graphics processing made possible by Nintendo's MMC (Memory Map Controller) chip, and the provision of battery-powered backup storage in Nintendo's new game cartridges allowed players to save their progress, thus making extended story lines more practical. The game interface also featured new elements, such as screens that were activated to manage the hero's items or abilities—a technique similar to the pull-down menus then beginning to appear in business software.

These innovations gave players freedom to navigate through a fully two-dimensional world (viewed from the top down) as Link's personality evolved through his efforts to defeat the evil Ganon and rescue Princess Zelda. Moreover, Miyamoto paid careful attention to the pacing and complexity of the game, ensuring that players would improve their skills as Link progressed to more difficult challenges. Success in *The Legend of Zelda* was measured by playing the game to completion over multiple sessions lasting perhaps dozens of hours, rather than scoring as many points as possible in a single session. Miyamoto thus raised expectations for greater narrative scope and more compelling game mechanics in a new generation of video games.

CHAPTER 2

NETWORKED GAMES AND NEXT-GENERATION CONSOLES

During the 1990s, computer game designers exploited three-dimensional graphics, faster microprocessors, networking, handheld and wireless game devices, and the Internet to develop new genres for video consoles, personal computers, and networked environments. These included first-person "shooters"—action games in which the environment is seen from the player's view—such as id Software's *Wolfenstein 3D* (1991), *Doom* (1993), and *Quake* (1996); sports games such as Electronic Arts' *Madden NFL* series (1989), based on motion-capture systems and artificial intelligence; and massively multiplayer games such as *Ultima Online* (1997), *EverQuest* (1999), and *World of Warcraft* (2004), combining traits of MUDs with graphical role-playing games to allow thousands of subscribers to create "avatars" (that is, representative icons or animated computer characters) and to explore "persistent" virtual worlds.

Communities of game players organized themselves around multiplayer teams (or "clans"), congregated on fan sites devoted to specific games, shared independent modifications (or "mods") of published games, or circulated their own player-made movies and replays ("machinima"). These groups shared common interests in computer game titles, using the Internet, broadband connections, LAN (local area network) parties, and other applications of networking technology in ways that increasingly merged in-game and out-of-game social experiences. New forms of participation challenged game developers to produce games that account for gamer communities and encourage player-created content. Examples of games that benefited from extending game play through the engagement of players included titles such as *The Sims* (2000) and *LittleBigPlanet* (2008).

ONLINE GAMING

Electronic gaming worlds generate billions of dollars as millions of players around the world fight, buy, craft, and sell in a variety of online environments. One of the most populous, Blizzard Entertainment's *World of Warcraft* (*WoW*), a massively multiplayer online game (MMOG), draws millions of subscribers, who bring the company an estimated $1 billion a year in retail sales and subscription fees.

MMOGs differ from traditional computer games in a number of important ways. First, Internet connectivity is a prerequisite for all MMOGs, as the games can be played only after logging in to the server that hosts the game world (popular MMOGs require dozens of such servers to accommodate their larger player bases). Second, the social networking aspect of interacting with thousands of players worldwide frequently overshadows the game content itself. A 2006 study found that almost a third of female players and nearly 10 percent of male players had dated someone they met in a game. Third, most MMOGs operate on a subscription basis, charging a monthly fee in addition to the initial purchase price of the game software. Some companies offer frequent downloadable "patches" of new game content to make these monthly fees more palatable to players, while others offer their games free of charge to players who are willing to tolerate a stream of in-game advertisements.

German gaming enthusiasts dress in character to promote the release of the World of Warcraft: Cataclysm *game in 2010. World of Warcraft* is one of the most popular gaming franchises. *Sean Gallup/Getty Images*

FROM MUDs TO MMOGs

Though *World of Warcraft* and other MMOGs utilize the advanced graphics and high-end processing power typical of the current generation of personal computers (PCs), online gaming had its roots in some of the earliest computing technologies. By the late 1970s, many universities in the United States were linked by ARPANET, a precursor to the Internet. The structure of ARPANET allowed users to connect their computers or terminals to a central mainframe computer and interact in what was close to real time. In 1980 ARPANET was linked to the University of Essex, Colchester, Eng., where two undergraduate students had written a text-based fantasy adventure game that they called *MUD* or "multiuser dungeon." When the first outside users connected to *MUD* through ARPANET, online gaming was born. Soon other programmers expanded on the original *MUD* design, adding graphic flourishes, chat functions, and player groups (or guilds). These basic features, as well as the fantasy setting, carried over into the next generation of online games, which were the first true MMOGs.

The first wave of MMOGs included such games as *Ultima Online* (debuted in 1997), the South Korean blockbuster *Lineage* (1998), and Sony Corporation's *EverQuest* (1999). Growth for these early games was relatively slow but steady with the exception of *Lineage*, the explosive popularity of which was mainly due to the early and widespread availability of high-speed Internet connections in South Korea. This popularity did not come without a price, however. A number of Korean players died of exhaustion after marathon gaming sessions, and a 2005 South Korean government survey showed that more than half a million Koreans suffered from "Internet addiction." Game companies funded dozens of private counseling centres for addicted gamers in an effort to forestall legislation, such as that passed by China in 2005, that would force designers to impose in-game penalties for players who spent more than three consecutive hours online.

By the time *World of Warcraft* debuted in November 2004, the global gaming market was ready for a change. With the notable exceptions of *EVE Online*, a game of interstellar corporate intrigue, and the superhero-themed *City of Heroes*, the market was saturated with "swords and sorcery" fare. *World of Warcraft*'s attention to humour and team play and its shallow learning curve brought in millions of casual gamers who had never before tried an MMOG. This widespread success brought its own challenges for Blizzard, however, when the company temporarily suspended the account of a transsexual player in 2006 over freedom of speech issues. While that incident seemed to have been the result of a terrible miscommunication on

Blizzard's part, it did open a dialogue on the nature of virtual reality worlds. Are they like private clubs, where the management can restrict both membership and speech? Or do they fall under the scope of a public accommodation, where discrimination is expressly prohibited by U.S. law?

Birth of Virtual Economies

Another issue that game publishers have had to face is the rise of secondary economies outside their game worlds. *Ultima Online* designers were the first to observe this phenomenon at work when a castle in their game world sold for several thousand dollars on the online auction site eBay. This was the beginning of a market valued at more than $1 billion by 2006.

Players spend hours earning in-game wealth, hunting for rare weapons, and gaining power and prestige for their characters so that the fruits of their virtual labours can be exchanged for real cash. The buyer and seller agree on a purchase price, the funds can be transferred electronically, and the two can then meet in the game world to complete the transaction. Some Chinese companies have turned this into serious business, employing "gold farmers," who play the game in an effort to hoard resources that can be sold to players in South Korea or the United States.

Most MMOG companies have sought to control this behaviour by banning the accounts of suspected gold farmers (e.g., Blizzard has closed tens of thousands of such accounts since *WoW* went online), and eBay began enforcing a ban on the sale of virtual items in 2007. Sony co-opted the secondary market when it launched Station Exchange, a service designed to facilitate the buying and selling of virtual goods in its *EverQuest* games. Linden Lab was the first company, however, to design a game around a virtual economy. That game was *Second Life*.

In many ways similar to *The Sims*, *Second Life* is less a game and more a virtual world. *The Sims Online* was a relative failure when it was introduced in late 2002, but *Second Life* became a runaway success soon after its launch in 2003. The difference was in the economic models adopted by the two games. Whereas *The Sims Online* was criticized for its lack of any clear goals for players, *Second Life* offered players the opportunity to use the game world and their own talents to make as much money as they possibly could. For a monthly subscription fee, players receive an allowance of Lindens (the in-game currency) that officially exchanges with U.S. dollars at a rate of approximately 250:1. Players can then purchase in-game items, customize those items by using 3D-imaging software, and resell them at a profit. For some, crafting items and managing virtual real estate in *Second Life* became a "first life" business.

GAMING COMMUNITIES AND SOCIAL GAMING

As electronic games have moved into the mainstream of commerce and culture around the world, developers of electronic games have explored social media as a new platform, incorporated technologies that rework the interactive and immersive aspects of gameplay, and applied game mechanics to many other fields of activity. The importance of social communities for online games emerged from the relatively closed worlds of MUDs and MMOGs with the massive global success of online games such as *Runescape* (2001) and *World of Warcraft*. Within a few years, these numbers were matched and exceeded by games produced for social networking services such as Facebook, notably Zynga's *Mafia Wars* (2008) and *Farmville* (2009) and Playfish's *Restaurant City* (2009).

The latest generation of home consoles introduced new technologies of motion control, most notably the Wii Remote for the Nintendo Wii system and the Kinect for Xbox 360. The cultural impact of electronic games throughout the world in the early 21st century was undeniable, paced by trends such as the growth and acceptance of game art, the "Serious Games" movement in education and training, and the controversial advocacy of "gamification," a term for the application of game mechanics to virtually any field of endeavour.

NOTABLE ONLINE GAMES

As high-speed Internet connections became more common, players were able to explore a variety of graphically rich, persistent game worlds. Fantasy settings were most prevalent, but science fiction and super-heroic milieus were also represented. Licensed games tied to specific works, such as *Star Wars*, *Star Trek*, or *Lord of the Rings*, allowed players to explore their favorite fictional universes.

Lineage

South Korean game developer NCsoft released *Lineage*, a multiplayer fantasy role-playing online game, in 1998. Although American versions of *Lineage* have been released, the game's core following is in South Korea, where the company boasted more than 3 million subscribers at the game's peak. *Lineage* allows players to battle one another or complete missions and develop their characters through castle siege or duel-style combat.

Lineage players begin by selecting a class of character. Playable types include elf, dark elf, knight, prince, and magician. Each class has different attributes and abilities, and each starts in a different area of the *Lineage* universe. As characters are developed, players form alliances, or blood pledges, to gain advantages in the game. *Lineage* features an advanced "marriage" system, in which players can obtain rings and complete a marriage ceremony. Being married allows a player to teleport to their spouse's location.

One of *Lineage*'s unique and enjoyable wrinkles is its pet system. Players can obtain pets of many types, ranging from killer rabbits to beagles, and train them to their specific needs. The real-life difficulty and time needed to train an animal is translated into the game. *Lineage* also sets itself apart from other similar games by putting increased focus on player-versus-player (PvP) combat. Released in 2003, *Lineage 2* — a prequel set 150 years before the action in *Lineage* — drew on many of the same elements that made the original game popular.

Second Life

Second Life, an Internet life-simulation network, was created in 2003 by the American company Linden Research, Inc. *Second Life* allows users to create and manage the lives of avatars they create in an advanced social setting with other online "residents."

Although it parallels a video game in some ways, *Second Life* lacks typical gaming objectives. Instead, it presents a world where users are able to create a persona and build a virtual life. This virtual life can entail hobbies, money, property, friends, and even sexual relationships. Real universities have hosted classes and lectures in the *Second Life* world, and additional developments have been researched to extend the program's educational uses. Currency in *Second Life* is the Linden Dollar, represented by L$, and it is sometimes exchanged for real money. Users are able to purchase virtual real estate, frequent virtual churches

Anshe Chung, an avatar in the virtually real world of Second Life.
Anshe Chung Studios

or clubs, and move about a sprawling virtual world as they please. The purchase of virtual real estate and property can be a substantial monetary investment (with real currency) and typically requires monthly upkeep fees.

There have been many instances of controversy throughout *Second Life*'s history. Accusations of unpunished theft and a lack of customer support have caused uproars among users, even leading high-profile residents to leave the game permanently. Furthermore, other scourges in the online world—such as riots between different social and political groups, bans on gambling and unlicensed banking, and ordinances to prevent the circulation of child pornography—indicate that even virtual worlds are not flawless.

World of Warcraft (WoW)

A massively multiplayer online role-playing game (MMORPG), *World of Warcraft*, or *WoW*, was created by the American company Blizzard Entertainment and was released on Nov. 14, 2004. Massively multiplayer refers to games in which thousands, even millions, of players may participate online together, typically in gaming worlds that persist indefinitely (with characters that are stored and then reactivated whenever a player rejoins). *WoW* is part of the *Warcraft* franchise, which includes *Warcraft: Orcs & Humans*, *Warcraft 2: Tides of Darkness*, and *Warcraft 3: Reign of Chaos*. Soon after its release, the game enjoyed a period of tremendous success and popularity among gamers worldwide.

Set in the fictional world of Azeroth, *WoW* allows players to create avatar-style characters and explore a sprawling universe while interacting with nonreal players—called nonplayer characters (NPCs)—and other real-world players (PCs). Various quests, battles, and missions are completed alone or in guilds, and the rewards for success include gold, weapons, and valuable items, which are used to improve one's character. Characters advance by killing other creatures to earn experience. Once enough experience is acquired, the character gains a level, which increases the character's powers. *WoW* offers a rich class system of characters, allowing gamers to play as druids, priests, rogues, paladins, and other fantasy-related classes. Guilds often achieve notoriety for their ability to finish certain quests or defeat specific monsters quickly, and, in this way, a hierarchy system is established in the game.

Players have contributed to the *WoW* community by creating artwork inspired by the game, writing fan fiction, and spending innumerable hours online inhabiting the game's virtual world. Some view this intense investment in the game as an addiction. There has been widespread abuse of *WoW*'s regenerating enemy population by users who employ autopilot programs or hire players to advance their characters at an unfairly rapid pace.

POPULAR HOME CONSOLES AND THE EXPANSION OF MOBILE GAMING

There were continuous improvements in home console technology through the 1990s, especially in graphics, storage, and controller technology. The next set of significant advances across a generation of video game consoles included the Sony Corporation's PlayStation 2 (2000) and Playstation 3 (2006–07), Nintendo's GameCube (2001) and Wii (2006), and the Microsoft Corporation's Xbox (2001) and Xbox 360 (2005). These consoles were defined in marketing and advertising primarily by their superior technology, especially 3D graphics and the exploitation of networking capabilities, which during the 1990s had been developed primarily for personal computer games.

Alongside the goal of intense, immersive experiences made possible by technical advances during the 1990s was mobile gaming. After the demonstrated success of purpose-built hardware such as the Game Boy, cell phones also gradually became viable platforms for electronic games, beginning with conversions of simple arcade games of an earlier era, such as *Snake*, released for Nokia phones in 1997. As the technical specifications of cell phones improved, games with color or 3D graphics were developed. The potential for cell phone games was enhanced by the possibility of integration with real-time, location-based tracking (such as GPS), messaging , and interaction with real-world events and places. The introduction of the Apple iPhone in 2007 and Apple's App Store in 2008 stabilized marketing and distribution of mobile games as cell phone applications; this business model was followed by developers who created games for other platforms, with varying degrees of success. Before long a few of the many small game developers that had moved to production of mobile games became major forces in the game industry, paced by Rovio Mobile, developer of the multiplatform blockbuster *Angry Birds* (2009).

NINTENDO CONSOLE

Japanese designer Uemura Masayuki created the groundbreaking eight-bit Nintendo console, or Nintendo Entertainment System (NES), which was released as the Famicom in Japan on July 15, 1983. The Famicom offered the ability to play popular arcade games such as *Donkey Kong* on a home television set and was extremely well received. The console's success in Japan triggered American interest, and negotiations began in order to bring the NES to the United States. After a 1985 showing at the Consumer Electronics Show and a limited release, the NES stormed America in February 1986 with titles such as *Duck Hunt*, *Hogan's Alley*, and, most famously, *Super Mario Bros.* More than 60 million NES consoles were sold, released, and distributed under various names and through several companies worldwide.

One of the NES's strengths was its library of games. *Super Mario Bros.* became the face of the system as gamers embraced Mario and Luigi, two plumbers who traveled through the Mushroom Kingdom to save Princess Toadstool from the evil Bowser. The *Mario Bros.* franchise went on to generate numerous sequels on the NES and other consoles. Another landmark title, *The Legend of Zelda*, also spawned many sequels. *The Legend of Zelda* franchise differs from game to game, but it usually focuses on the adventures of Link, a green-clad, sword-toting hero, in his quest to save Princess Zelda.

The NES eventually faded from the spotlight as new 16-bit consoles were created, such as the Sega Genesis and Nintendo's own Super Nintendo Entertainment System. However, games were still released for the NES into the 1990s, until licensed production on a library of more than 1,000 titles ceased in 1994. The NES, though less technologically advanced than newer consoles, remained a popular choice of "retro" gamers into the 21st century.

NINTENDO WII

After the Nintendo 64 (1996) and Nintendo GameCube (2001) failed to achieve the market dominance that the NES had, Nintendo took a different course for its next home console, the Wii. Instead of directly competing (in terms of processing power and graphics display) with rival video consoles such as the Xbox 360 and PlayStation 3 (PS3), Nintendo produced an innovative, low-cost console that featured multiplayer "party" games. While the Xbox 360 and the PS3 were fighting over the traditional, or "hard-core," gamers, the Wii, which debuted in the United States and Japan in 2006, broadened the entire video game console market. In the process, it established a large user base.

The Wii's innovations began with its controllers, which were wireless remotes that attached to a joystick or other input device. The remote keyed into a wireless sensor attached to the console so that the games detected movement of the device as well as input from the device's buttons. For example, people playing the tennis game in *Wii Sports* would swing their arms, rather than push buttons, to hit the ball. A variety of different controllers were available, such as a balance board, a racing wheel, and a

Professional tennis player Andy Roddick tests his skills at the electronic version of the game using Nintendo's Wii console at a Bloomingdales department store promotional event in 2008. Jemal Countess/WireImage/Getty Images

floor mat. The Wii's specialty was group play, with a wide range of games and modes that were simple enough for inexperienced gamers but enjoyable enough for hard-core gamers. Wii parties helped generate consumer demand for the system, which resulted in market shortages for the console and some of its games during several holiday seasons in the United States.

The Wii also had built-in Wi-Fi for connecting to the Internet. After a connection was established with one of Nintendo's special servers, players could choose from various channels to communicate and play with other Wii owners, display news and weather reports, download from an extensive online library of classic Nintendo games from older systems, and create and display special Wii avatars, known as Miis. A browser could also be purchased for surfing the World Wide Web.

In July 2009 Nintendo released a peripheral adapter, known as the Wii MotionPlus, for the Wii remote control. The device plugged into the base of the original remote and added more-precise tracking of the remote's position and orientation. In addition to being sold separately, the adapter was packaged with *Wii Sports Resort*, which included air sports, archery, basketball, bowling, canoeing, cycling, frisbee, golf, power cruising, skydiving, swordplay, table tennis, and wakeboarding.

PLAYSTATION

The PlayStation, released in 1994, was one of a new generation of 32-bit consoles, and it signaled Sony's rise to power in the video game world. Also known as the PS One, the PlayStation used compact discs (CDs), heralding the video game industry's move away from cartridges.

After a failed venture with Nintendo to release the PlayStation as the Super Nintendo Entertainment System–CD in the early 1990s, Sony made the decision to market its own console. The PlayStation was released in Japan in December 1994, and it made its American debut in September 1995; both releases elicited critical acclaim and impressive sales. Titles such as *Twisted Metal* and *Ridge Racer* were very popular. By 2005 the PlayStation had become the first console ever to ship 100 million units. PlayStation's premier games included fan favourites such as *Final Fantasy 7*, *Crash Bandicoot*, and *Tekken*, all of which spawned numerous sequels.

The original PlayStation continued production until March 2005, when it was eclipsed by the next generation of 64-bit consoles, including Sony's own PlayStation 2 (PS2). Introduced in the early 2000s, the PS2 offered the ability to play over the Internet, which, combined with an extensive line of games, led to its sales dominance over its

PLAYSTATION HOME

PlayStation Home was a network-based service that allowed users of the Sony Corporation's PlayStation 3 (PS3) electronic-game console to interact in a computer-generated virtual community.

PlayStation Home uses a video game–like interface to present a socially interactive environment. Players connect via their gaming console to the online PlayStation Network (PSN) to access Home, design an avatar, decorate a virtual apartment (or "HomeSpace"), and venture out into the larger video world. In the central Home Square, players in numerous physical locations encounter one another's avatars, converse by way of text "bubbles" over their characters' heads, play games such as chess and bowling, and explore a variety of rooms, shops, and events. Players can direct their avatars to perform a number of different gestures, dances, and other actions.

Access to the Home environment is free for PSN subscribers, as are many basic clothing items, home furnishings, and decorations that players can use for their avatars and in their HomeSpaces. Players can purchase more elaborate virtual items, or even larger HomeSpaces, from Sony in online stores. A Home Theater shows video content, including trailers for upcoming movies and games. Home is used to promote PlayStation games by way of themed rooms and visual advertising; Sony plans to eventually license similar promotions for other products.

Sony first announced plans for Home in early 2007, seeking to gain a market advantage for its PS3 console over competitors. However, the project was delayed several times, with a public trial, or "beta," version finally debuting in December 2008. The beta was released in multiple languages in the United States, Europe, Japan, and elsewhere, each with its own local Home network.

64-bit rivals Sega Dreamcast and Nintendo GameCube. In fact, PlayStation 2 went on to ship 100 million units faster than any of its predecessors or contemporaries. However, the next installment of the PlayStation consoles, the PlayStation 3 (released in 2006 and 2007), did not enjoy the same initial success as the earlier incarnations of the console, with ongoing competition from the Microsoft Xbox 360 and the Nintendo Wii.

Xbox

Concerned about Sony's successful PlayStation console damaging the personal computer market, Microsoft initiated plans in 1999 to create its own console gaming system to both diversify its product line and capitalize on the thriving gaming industry. The system—originally termed the DirectX-box for its use of the eponymous video software—underwent multiple launch delays. The Xbox, Microsoft's first entry into the world of console electronic gaming, was released in 2001, which placed it in direct competition with Sony's PlayStation 2 and Nintendo's GameCube. The Xbox underwent several pricing adjustments after it made its debut.

Despite popular titles such as *Halo: Combat Evolved* and *Halo 2*, Microsoft reported in 2005 that it had thus far lost $4 billion from the Xbox enterprise. Xbox offered superior technological features (as compared with its competitors), but it initially lacked some of the software licensing benefits available to rivals Nintendo and Sony. Xbox Live, the Xbox's online gaming network, debuted in 2002 and allowed players to compete against one another over the Internet. Millions of players subscribed to Xbox Live, establishing it as one of the Xbox's greatest successes. Many people exploited security flaws in the Xbox to modify the system so that pirated copies of games could be played on the console, a process that was popular despite the fact that such alterations voided the warranty.

In 2005 the Xbox was replaced by Microsoft's Xbox 360, yet many players continued to use the original Xbox and take advantage of the Xbox Live network. Hardware modification and software piracy remained an issue with the Xbox 360, but Microsoft took the dramatic step of banning one million accounts from the Xbox Live network in 2009 when it detected that those users had circumvented the company's digital-rights management protections.

In an intensely competitive market, where the Xbox 360 faced strong pressure from the Nintendo Wii and the Sony PlayStation, Microsoft struggled to make consistent profits from its console. For example, in 2009 Microsoft cut the price of the Xbox 360 Elite by as much as 25 percent in order to pick up market share. The move was successful. By 2010 the Xbox 360 was the most-used game console in the American home, and the Xbox Live network boasted more than 20 million subscribers.

CHAPTER 3

ELECTRONIC
SHOOTER GAMES

In the electronic shooter game genre, players control a character or unit that wields weapons to shoot enemies. While shooting games involving "light guns" and photoreceptors were experimented with as early as the 1930s, the birth of this genre of electronic games really began in 1962 with *Spacewar!*, a software program developed to show off the power of the Digital Equipment Corporation PDP-1 minicomputer. The game included stellar objects that generated gravitation fields, which two players had to take into account as they maneuvered their spacecraft while shooting at each other and various asteroids. American computer programmers Nolan Bushnell and Ted Dabney simplified the game to one person shooting alien spaceships, and this version was published by Nutting Associates as *Computer Space* (1971), the first mass-produced coin-operated electronic game, or arcade game. Bushnell and Dabney later founded Atari Inc., from which they released the first commercially successful arcade game, *Pong* (1972), an electronic sports game based on table tennis, colloquially known as Ping-Pong.

Although *Computer Space* had too steep a learning curve to prove a commercial success, the same cannot be said of *Space Invaders* (1978). An arcade console produced by Taito Corporation in Japan and licensed to Bally Technologies in the United States, *Space Invaders* was

A visitor to Germany's Computer Game Museum plays a vintage Space Invaders *arcade game, 2011. Immensely popular worldwide,* Space Invaders *was the first video game licensed for use on home gaming consoles.* Sean Gallup/Getty Images

an enormous hit—so much so that Japan experienced a temporary shortage of 100-yen coins, which were used there to play the game. In 1980 *Space Invaders* became the first arcade game to be licensed for a home gaming console, the Atari 2600. Atari also released *Asteroids* (1979) and *Missile Command* (1980) as arcade games before they made their way to home console machines and personal computers (PCs).

THE SHOOTER GAME GENRE

While early shooters generally had limited player mobility, typically involving nothing more than allowing the player to move a weapon horizontally or vertically along the edges of the screen, increased computer power enabled the development of games played from a first-person perspective. Typically, in first-person shooter games, players move through mazelike corridors and rooms filled with adversaries—controlled by other players or the computer—and via stealth or more accurate shooting try to outlive their opponents.

Although *Wolfenstein 3-D* (1992), produced by id Software for PCs, was not the original first-person shooter (FPS) game, it set the standard for the subgenre. *Doom* (1993), the followup game from id Software, was the first FPS game with multiplayer support. Other popular FPS games released in the 1990s included *Duke Nukem 3D* (1996), *Quake* (1996), *Half-Life* (1998), and *Unreal Tournament* (1999). This subgenre in particular has driven the development of the PC market, with players often rushing to upgrade or replace their PCs in order to handle ever more realistic game engines.

Although multiplayer combat remains as popular as ever, as evidenced by the success of such games as Valve's *Team Fortress 2* (2007) and Activision's *Call of Duty: Black Ops* (2010), the market for pure single-player FPS games has declined in favour of games that blend elements from other genres. Successful variations on the FPS include the electronic adventure games *Half-Life*, *Half-Life 2* (2004), and *BioShock*, which incorporate horror or survival elements and more complex story lines. Valve was also responsible for *Portal* (2007) and *Portal 2* (2011), a pair of first-person puzzle games that feature a darkly comic plot and wildly innovative game that uses first-person shooter conventions and control schemes.

NOTABLE SHOOTER GAMES

From *Spacewar!* to *Space Invaders*, from *Doom* to *Call of Duty*, this genre has contained some of the most innovative, addictive, and, occasionally, controversial titles in the history of electronic games.

Space Invaders

One of the earliest video games released and one of the most influential electronic games of all time, *Space Invaders* was created by Japanese engineer and game designer Nishikado Tomohiro in 1978, and produced by Japanese manufacturer Taito Corp. The objective of *Space Invaders* was to pan across a screen and shoot descending swarms of aliens, preventing them from reaching the bottom of the screen. It is viewed as a pioneer of modern gaming.

A very simple game by modern standards, *Space Invaders* had been considered a technological marvel in its time. Typical levels consist of a player piloting a laser cannon to battle columns of descending aliens while using shields to block alien fire. The speed of the alien approach increases as the game progresses, adding to the tension. A bonus alien spaceship appears from time to time, which offers the player an opportunity to score additional points by blowing it up.

Space Invaders was a worldwide success and paved the way for a generation of shooting games that became extremely popular. In 1980 American game manufacturer Atari, Inc., adapted a version of the game for the Atari 2600 console, fueling the popularity of home gaming. Countless sequels, spin-offs, and releases of *Space Invaders* have been generated over the years, including Taito's *Space Raiders* (2003). In 2008, in celebration of the game's 30th anniversary, Nintendo released *Space Invaders Get Even*, an online game available in Japan for the company's Wii console, in which players control the invading aliens, rather than the defending laser cannon.

Doom

Doom, an innovative first-person shooter, was released in December 1993 and changed the direction of almost every aspect of personal computer (PC) games, from graphics and networking technology to styles of play, notions of authorship, and public scrutiny of game content.

John Carmack (far right) poses with fellow software developers at the 2005 Los Angeles premiere of Doom. *The game's 3D graphics and innovative playing style revolutionized PC gaming.* Albert L. Ortega/WireImage/Getty Images

The authors of *Doom* were a group of programmers, led by John Romero and John Carmack, formed in Texas to create monthly games as employees of *Softdisk* magazine. While at *Softdisk* the group also produced shareware titles for Apogee Software, beginning with the *Commander Keen* franchise (1990–91). On the basis of the success of this series of addictive platform games, the group formed id Software in February 1991.

From the beginning, id focused on the development of superior graphics. Carmack had already demonstrated, by writing a smooth-scrolling PC version of Nintendo's *Super Mario Brothers 3*, that personal computers could rival video consoles. Now he turned his attention to three-dimensional gaming graphics, writing a "graphics engine" for id's *Wolfenstein 3D*, an action game published by Apogee, that depicted the environment as the player's character would see it. This set the stage for *Doom* as the next step of the first-person shooter game genre. *Doom* added numerous technical and design improvements to the *Wolfenstein 3D* model: a superior graphics engine, fast peer-to-peer networking for multiplayer gaming, a modular design that let authors outside id create new levels, and a new mode of competitive play devised by Romero called "death match."

The game's plot was an immersive mix of science fiction and horror. The player, seeing through the eyes of an unidentified space marine, is sent to investigate an incident on the Martian moon Phobos. Humanlike opponents give way to increasingly demonic enemies as the player punches, shoots, and chainsaws through an array of hellish settings. The game was a phenomenal success—it contributed so much to the genre that, initially, all similar titles were referred to as "Doom clones," and it immediately established competitive multiplayer gaming as a critical element in future PC titles. At the same time, the subject matter of *Doom* (slaughtering demons in outer space), its moody graphics and audio (combined with realistic depictions of blood and gore), and its vocabulary (such as "shooters" and "death match") focused public attention on the level of violence depicted in computer games.

After succeeding with the first installment of the series, id Software released *Doom II: Hell on Earth* in 1994. In 1997 the U.S. Marine Corps converted *Doom*'s monsters into opposition forces and used the resulting game, *Marine Doom*, to train troops in tactics and communications. After the series went on hiatus through the late 1990s, *Doom 3* was released to great critical acclaim in 2004. In 2005 the popular video game title was made into a motion picture of the same name.

Half-Life

American game developer Sierra Studios released *Half-Life* in 1998 for personal computers and in 2001 for the Sony Corporation's PlayStation 2 video game console. One of the most popular and critically acclaimed games of the late 1990s, *Half-Life* followed theoretical physicist Gordon Freeman as he blasted his way through a research facility where his own experiments had gone horribly wrong.

Half-Life differed from other first-person shooter games by moving away from cinematic plot devices, instead telling the story through live scripted interactions. A massive array of weaponry was available to help players "mow down" aliens, mutants, assassins, and marines. Rather than simply trading gunfire while running around, *Half-Life* required players to manipulate and use parts of the research facility to destroy the more difficult enemies. The game was filled with puzzles, a departure from the standard "shoot-'em-up" genre, and play was organized by chapters rather than levels.

NVIDIA CORPORATION

The desire for added realism in first-person shooters drove the development of vastly more powerful graphics processors—which, in turn, inspired programmers to push the limits of those processors. NVIDIA, a global corporation that manufactures graphics processors, mobile technologies, and desktop computers, was at the forefront of these developments. The company was founded in 1993 by three American computer scientists, Jen-Hsun Huang, Curtis Priem, and Christopher Malachowsky. NVIDIA is known for developing integrated circuits used in everything from electronic game consoles to personal computers. Headquartered in Santa Clara, Calif., the company also is a leading manufacturer of high-end graphics processing units (GPUs).

NVIDIA became a major force in the computer gaming industry with the launch of the RIVA series of graphics processors in 1997. Two years later, the company gained prominence with the release of the GeForce 256 GPU, which offered superior three-dimensional graphics quality. NVIDIA battled with prominent video card maker 3dfx Interactive, pitting the GeForce against 3dfx Interactive's popular Voodoo technologies. NVIDIA eventually prevailed and purchased 3dfx Interactive's remaining assets in 2000. That same year, Microsoft Corporation selected NVIDIA to develop graphics cards for Microsoft's long-awaited Xbox video game console. In 2007, NVIDIA was honoured as Company of the Year by *Forbes* magazine for its rapid growth and success.

In 1998 *Half-Life* won more than 50 game of the year awards from various Web sites and magazines. The innovations found in *Half-Life* helped breathe new life into a genre that had been made famous by *Doom*, *Quake*, and *Wolfenstein*, and its multiplayer support made it one of the most-played online games. The *Guinness Book of World Records* named it the Best-Selling First-Person Shooter of All Time (PC) in 2008.

Half-Life 2, the game's direct sequel, was released in 2004 for PCs; the game was later ported to Xbox and Xbox 360 video game consoles and PlayStation 3. The game, which chronicled new battles in a world wrecked by the residual effects of the first *Half-Life* game, experienced widespread success similar to that of its predecessor. *Half-Life 2* featured several expansion packs that extended the story in what many viewed as an unofficial third installment of the series.

Unreal Tournament

Unreal Tournament, a first-person shooter game, was released by American game developer GT Interactive Software Corp. (now Atari, Inc.) in 1999. A sequel to the popular combat video game *Unreal*, *Unreal Tournament* represented a shift from single-player action to multiplayer online gaming. The game received critical acclaim for its superior graphics and advanced gameplay, and for offering one of the first team shooter games.

Set in deep space, *Unreal Tournament* takes place in a distant future in which gladiator-style fights have been legalized. Players compete in tournaments using advanced weaponry and accomplish the goal of the particular game mode or mission while causing maximum carnage. Cooperative and team-play options are high points of *Unreal Tournament*, along with an advanced artificial intelligence engine. Available play modes include Deathmatch, Team Deathmatch, Domination, Last Man Standing, and Assault. Gore, long a trademark of the shooter genre, has plenty of representation in the game.

Unreal Tournament's popularity led to several well-received sequels: *Unreal Tournament 2003* (2002), *Unreal Tournament 2004* (2004), and *Unreal Tournament 3* (2007). The popular and enduring franchise has inspired fans to create their own levels and features for the game using the original *Unreal Tournament* codes. These user-created modifications, known as mods, can be found at various Web sites and message boards on the Internet.

Halo

Halo, a first-person shooter game, was developed by Bungie Studios and released in 2001 by the Microsoft Corporation for its Xbox console. Using state-of-the-art graphics, sophisticated genre improvements, and an array of weapons and vehicles, *Halo*'s first release, *Combat Evolved*, was a resounding triumph that helped make the launch of the Xbox a success in the console gaming market.

In *Halo*, players control Master Chief, a super soldier who is trying to uncover the mystery of a strange object, the Halo. The majority of enemies a player encounters are a part of the Covenant, an alien race bent on destruction. The Covenant is broken up into several classes, which include grunts, elites, hunters, and jackals, all of which have certain tendencies, weaknesses, and strengths. Players also encounter the Flood, a parasitic alien that takes over human and Covenant soldiers and causes havoc. Gamers are often flanked by computer-controlled allies who provide covering fire and support in tough battles. By allowing players to use a variety of items and weaponry in different situations, *Halo* won fans with a system that was easy to learn but also skill-intensive enough to provide a challenge for veteran gamers.

Viewed as one of the most important video game releases in history, the first version of *Halo* sold more than 5 million copies and spawned a number of sequels. Multiplayer game play, a weak point of the first release, was greatly improved in *Halo 2* (2004), which quickly became one of the most popular titles on the Xbox Live online play network. *Halo 3* (2007) concluded the story of Master Chief and continued the franchise's success, grossing more than $300 million in the first week of its release. *Halo: Reach* (2010) introduced a new cast of characters—the elite military force Noble Team—in a single-player story line that served as a prequel to the original *Combat Evolved*. With highly customizable game play and a robust multiplayer matchmaking system that integrated aspects of social networking sites, *Halo: Reach* was hugely popular, with more than $200 million in global sales in the first 24 hours after its release.

America's Army

The first-person shooter game *America's Army* is unique because it is first and foremost an army training simulator and recruitment tool. Created in 2002 by Lt. Col. Casey Wardynski, the game is maintained and managed by the United States Army. It received positive reviews for its realistic depiction of a soldier's experiences. Millions of registered users have contributed to the game's success since its release.

America's Army was conceived as a way to generate interest in the army and recruit tech-savvy video game enthusiasts. The game is free via download over the Internet, or it can be obtained at army recruitment centres. The game is played online, where it enjoys a large community of loyal followers. *America's Army* has evolved to the point where it is utilized as a training tool by the U.S. Army to prepare recruits for particular combat scenarios. Game play centres on passing a series of training courses before moving on to simulated combat scenarios. Players can choose what type of soldier they would like to be and are then given a series of tasks to complete in order to achieve that goal. To be a medic, for instance, players must pass a combat medic training simulator. The game is so realistic that it helped *America's Army* enthusiast Paxton Galvanek rescue and treat two car accident victims in 2007 despite having no medical training outside of what he had learned from the game.

America's Army has won numerous awards. The game has been criticized, however, for not showing the true gore and mayhem of war, opting instead to maintain a teen-friendly rating from the Entertainment Software Rating Board. Major expansions, released in 2003 and 2009, refined gameplay and emphasized non-traditional shooter game tasks such as intelligence gathering and forward observation.

Call of Duty

The *Call of Duty* franchise brought new advances to the first-person shooter genre, winning numerous game of the year awards following its 2003 debut. Designed by the American company Infinity Ward and produced by Activision, the first *Call of Duty* used World War II as a setting, allowing players to see the war through the eyes of American, Soviet, and British soldiers. *Call of Duty* combined challenging single-player missions with a multiplayer engine that breathed new life into a genre spawned by such gaming greats as *Doom* and *Quake*.

Call of Duty allowed players to advance through World War II in a series of campaigns or to battle it out against human opponents in its multiplayer mode. Solo play featured a cast of computer-controlled allies to better simulate actual war, during which a soldier would have been part of a large group rather than always fighting alone. The ability to pull up and aim firearms, relive the last few seconds of a fallen comrade's life, and realistically be stunned by nearby explosions were notable features that helped distance the game from its competitors.

The popularity of *Call of Duty* spawned multiple sequels and expansions, such as *Call of Duty II*, *Call of Duty: Finest Hour*, and *Call of Duty III*. The series explored new ground in 2007 when *Call of Duty 4: Modern Warfare* was released, giving players the chance to immerse themselves

Shoppers snap up copies of Call of Duty: Black Ops, *the seventh install-*
ment of the franchise, at a midnight release event in 2010. Ethan Miller/
Getty Images

in a fantasy future conflict among the United States, the
United Kingdom, and Russia. A hit with players and critics alike, *Modern Warfare* was the best-selling game of 2007
and helped the series maintain its place at the top of the
war-game genre. Its sequel, *Call of Duty: Modern Warfare
2*, set entertainment industry records during its first five
days of release in November 2009, grossing more than
$550 million in worldwide sales. The game's single-player
mode featured a deeply engaging counterterrorism sto-
ryline, and its robust multiplayer mode drew more than 2
million users to Xbox Live, marking a one-day record for
the online gaming service.

The franchise's next release, *Call of Duty: Black Ops*, topped $360 million in sales on its first day of release in November 2010, easily becoming the largest entertainment opening of the year. The game featured a single-player story rooted in the events of the Cold War, offering an evenly balanced, heavily customizable multiplayer mode.

Far Cry

German developer Crytek created its CryENGINE 3D rendering technology for a number of applications, but it is perhaps best known for its use in the first-person shooter *Far Cry*. Released for personal computers in 2004 by Ubisoft Entertainment SA, an entertainment-software company based in France, *Far Cry* enjoyed strong sales and impressed critics with its mix of stealth and "shoot-'em-up" first-person action. The game also was noted for its superior graphics, which featured realistic lighting and a highly detailed depiction of the game's island setting. The latter eschewed the dark, cramped corridors of many shooter games, replacing them with an open, lush, jungle environment.

Far Cry's story centres on Jack Carver, a former member of the Special Forces who winds up stranded on an island in Micronesia searching for a missing journalist named Val Cortez. Krieger, a demented scientist who has been tinkering with genetic engineering, has let loose on the island mutated monsters that Carver must navigate through to rescue Cortez. *Far Cry* was praised for being unusually long for the first-person shooter genre, offering challenges that required more than point-and-shoot reflexes and featuring a wide variety of environments to explore. Because the artificial intelligence incorporated into the game was much better than that in comparable games, players had to find creative solutions in situations in which they were outnumbered or outgunned. The game also featured a checkpoint-saving system that eliminated manual saving, a multiplayer option, and a level creator (for users to add more content).

In Germany, the Federal Department for Media Harmful to Young Persons, a media watchdog group, deemed *Far Cry*'s violence too brutal and demanded that it be edited. Even with significant changes to the game, it received a +18 age rating in Germany. *Far Cry*'s popularity led to the release of *Far Cry 2*, a sequel in name only that did not follow the original's story, though it still earned outstanding reviews.

BioShock

BioShock was a computer and console electronic game created by game developer 2k Boston/2k Australia and released in 2007. *BioShock* impressed critics with its detailed story line and innovative play, which helped earn the game a coveted top-20 slot on GameRankings.com, a Web site that tracks game reviews and ratings across the Internet. The game contains elements of the popular *System Shock* series of games, which was created by the same development team.

BioShock puts players in the shoes of Jack, who survives an airplane crash and sets out to explore a city that has been submerged in water. The game takes place in a demented version of 1960, where players battle mutated, armour-clad humans known as Big Daddies. Little Sisters, a primary source of energy in the game, are protected by the Daddies and can either be killed for their resources or rescued. This wrinkle introduces an element of morality into the game and influences the story line. By gathering items known as mutagens, players can mutate and develop useful abilities such as telekinesis. An array of special weapons and other items are also available.

An ambitious project that managed to successfully combine elements from the first-person shooter, stealth, and role-playing game genres, *BioShock* won Spike TV's 2007 Best Game award and X-Play's 2007 Game of the Year award. In addition to critical acclaim, *BioShock* enjoyed commercial success, and a sequel, *BioShock 2*, was released in 2010.

CHAPTER 4

ELECTRONIC
SPORTS GAMES

The electronic sports game genre simulates a real or imagined sport. The first commercial electronic sports game, as well as the first commercially successful arcade game, was *Pong* (1972). Produced by the American company Atari Inc., *Pong* was a simulation of table tennis (Ping-Pong).

THE SPORTS GAME GENRE

Since its founding in 1982, the American company Electronic Arts, and in particular EA Sports, has been the premier developer of electronic sports games for personal computers and video game consoles. Among its marquee sports titles are *John Madden Football/Madden NFL* (1988–), *PGA Tour/Tiger Woods PGA Tour* (1990–), *NHL* (1991–), *FIFA* (1993–), *Bill Walsh College Football/NCAA Football* (1993–), *NBA Live* (1994–), and *Triple Play/MVP Baseball* (1996–).

EA Sports maintains its market dominance through annual sequels that typically include actual player names and likenesses, often licensed on an exclusive basis. Incremental improvements in fidelity to realism has extended to using videos of the players to model their game movements.

The cover of the 2010 installment of EA Sports' Tiger Woods PGA Tour *video game. EA Sports licenses the use of sports figure names and likenesses for its games.* © AP Images

The Nintendo Company's Wii (2006) home video console, with its motion-sensitive controllers, enabled a new way of playing electronic sports games. In particular, the launch title *Wii Sports* (2006), which included baseball, bowling, boxing, golf, and tennis, appealed to a much wider demographic than any previous electronic game and soon created something of a fad for *Wii Sports* parties at which family and friends competed against one another.

ELECTRONIC ARTS, INC.

Electronic Arts (EA) is an American developer and manufacturer of electronic games for personal computers (PCs) and video game consoles and is one of the largest companies in the industry. Established in 1982 by William M. ("Trip") Hawkins, EA now has a product line that includes the popular franchises *The Sims, Command & Conquer,* and *Madden NFL.* The company is headquartered in Redwood City, Calif.

Hawkins had been employed by Apple Inc. but left in 1982 to found Amazin' Software, which was renamed Electronic Arts later that year. One of EA's unique features was the amount of recognition it gave to game designers, placing their names in large type on some game covers, similar to novel or album cover designs.

EA's titles encompass a broad range of genres and game types. In 1997 EA acquired Maxis Software, makers of *SimCity,* and continued the Maxis label for several years as the developer of various sequels, including *The Sims,* the best-selling PC game of all time. In 2008 EA's Maxis studios produced *Spore,* a game in which users create and evolve life forms in a virtual world. *Medal of Honor, Ultima Online, Rock Band, Burnout,* and the *Battlefield* franchise also are part of EA's extensive library.

NOTABLE SPORTS GAMES

Electronic sports games got their start with a simple yet addictive Ping-Pong simulator, but they now include digital adaptations of any individual or team sport imaginable. The key word is "imaginable," as some games represent sports that exist only in works of fiction, such as Quidditch (from the *Harry Potter* series) or pod racing (from *Star Wars*).

Madden NFL

A sports-simulation series, *Madden NFL* was based on the National Football League (NFL). Its name derives from John Madden, a famous football coach and television colour commentator. EA Sports has held exclusive licensing rights with the NFL since 2005, making *Madden NFL* the only American football video game available with all the NFL teams and their players.

Madden NFL originated in 1989 as *John Madden Football*, a computer software title for the Apple II. The franchise was popularized with a move to the Sega Genesis console in 1990 and the Super Nintendo Entertainment System in 1991. The name was changed to *Madden NFL* in 1993, when it gained full licensing and began releasing titles corresponding to each NFL season for multiple gaming consoles.

In the early 21st century, *Madden NFL* developed innovative game-play modes to heighten realism and expand

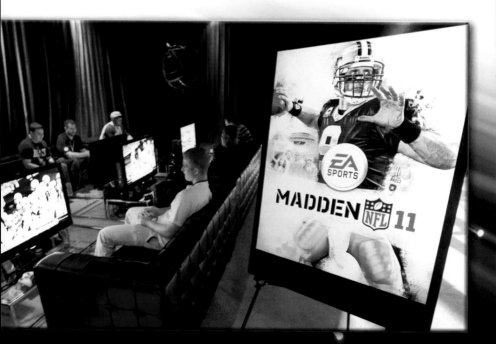

Players test the 2011 version of EA Sports' Madden NFL *game. Begun in 1989, the franchise has added heightened realism and innovative game play to each of its successive editions.* Bloomberg via Getty Images

on the NFL gaming experience. The ability to create and manage an NFL franchise, assemble a playbook, and design a stadium were well received. Also, advances in realistic player movement and mechanics enhanced the game's appeal. However, as other video game software companies were legally forced to discontinue NFL titles, there was controversy over EA's incentive to continue to improve upon the series in a market where it had no competitors. Despite these concerns, *Madden NFL 2007* broke sales records after selling more than 3.9 million copies, further establishing the franchise's dominance in NFL gaming.

FIFA

The *FIFA* soccer series was developed by EA Sports, a division of the American gaming company Electronic Arts, and licensed from the Fédération Internationale de Football Association (FIFA). EA Sports began the *FIFA* series in 1993, hoping to develop a hold on soccer in the same way that they dominated the market for American football gaming with *Madden NFL*.

Starting with *FIFA International Soccer*, EA Sports created a handful of additions for 16-bit electronic game systems and the Sega CD. Unfortunately, the game included only national teams and was plagued by a bug that allowed for easy goal scoring. *FIFA Soccer 95* was released for personal computers and the Sega Mega Drive. *FIFA Soccer 96* was the first in the series to offer real-time three-dimensional play on the systems of the time. *FIFA* titles released by EA Sports seemed to lag behind the competition in some game-play aspects, however, until a series of overhauls in 2006 improved the control of the game and presented new features such as an in-depth career mode, which adds various coaching features.

The primary series has been flanked by other installments based on major soccer tournaments, such as the FIFA World Cup and UEFA Champions League, as well as a series of other soccer titles. *FIFA 08* saw the implementation of the Be a Pro feature, as well as the ability to play on Nintendo's Wii console, opening up a new world of control options using the Wii's motion-sensing remote, which allows players to interact with the game by pointing and moving the remote.

Wii Sports

Japanese designer Eguchi Katsuya created *Wii Sports* for the 2006 launch of the Nintendo Wii video game console. *Wii Sports* features five individual games that showcase the

A gaming show attendee tries out a new EA Sports game, NFL Training Camp, *designed exclusively for the Wii console. Nintendo's* Wii Sports *features five sports other than football. Bloomberg via Getty Images*

Wii Fit

Wii Fit was an interactive fitness game that was released in 2007 by the Nintendo Company Ltd. for their Wii gaming system.

Wii Fit consists of software along with a balance board that enables users to do an extensive series of yoga exercises. For more aggressive fitness enthusiasts, *Wii Fit* offers strength training and aerobics activities. In addition, casual players can engage in a series of games, such as tightrope walking, skiing, and snowboarding. Activities are documented in a virtual logbook, which helps users monitor and track their progress.

Wii Fit was a commercial success in nearly every market where it was introduced, often selling out the available inventory within days of its release. Despite its popularity, critics of the game claimed that it did not offer a serious workout regimen: game menu breaks prevent the sustained elevated heart rates necessary for improving cardiovascular health, and the ability to cheat on certain exercises can present a false impression of progress. According to the game's Japanese designer, Miyamoto Shigeru, the *Wii Fit* has the potential to connect physical therapists and personal trainers with their clients over the Internet.

Wii's unique motion-sensitive controller, which translates a player's actual actions with the controller into actions by a character, or avatar, in the game. The easy nature of *Wii Sports'* controls and its social elements encouraged gaming parties, which helped fuel the successful launch of the Wii console.

Wii Sports includes golf, bowling, boxing, baseball, and tennis games. Players use the Wii's wireless motion-sensitive remote to mimic the actions used when playing real-life games. In the baseball game, for instance, a player swings the controller to produce the swing of the bat on-screen. Abandoning the graphic violence that has dominated the industry, *Wii Sports* offers a very simple and tranquil setting for its games and adds a social element to the gaming experience by encouraging group play. One of

Wii Sports' unique features is the ability to integrate avatars designed with the Mii character creation system into the game. Mii character creation allows players to make an avatar, starting from a few customizable cartoonlike characters, or to import characters made elsewhere (e.g., on a computer). A personal avatar can then be used as the player's on-screen presence in games.

Wii Sports was designed to attract people who had not previously played video games, creating a medium where dedicated and experienced game players could interact with neophytes. Although the game has been generally well-received, the simple and user-friendly interface can be boring to some more experienced players.

CHAPTER 5

ELECTRONIC ADVENTURE GAMES

The electronic adventure game genre is characterized by exploring, puzzle solving, narrative interactions with game characters, and, for action-adventure games, running, jumping, climbing, fighting, and other intense action sequences. Many modern electronic games, such as role-playing games (RPGs) and shooter games, contain some adventure characteristics, making precise categorization impossible.

TEXT-BASED ADVENTURES

The first electronic adventure game was Will Crowther's *Adventure* (c. 1977) for the Digital Equipment Corporation PDP-10 minicomputer. This text-based adventure, often referred to as interactive fiction, became the prototype for later games such as *Zork* (1977), which was written by students at the Massachusetts Institute of Technology for the school's computer system.

GRAPHIC-BASED ADVENTURES

The next step in the evolution of the basic genre is usually credited to writer Roberta Williams and her computer programmer husband, Ken Williams, who formed Sierra Entertainment (1979). In particular, beginning with *King's*

Quest (1984) for MS-DOS, Sierra released a steady stream of successful graphical adventure games throughout the 1980s and early '90s. While the graphics consisted of nothing more than colourful static images that players could "point-and-click" on to load text or other screens, it was the interactive fiction elements in Roberta Williams's stories that enthralled fans. The company's other best-known titles were *Space Quest* (1986), *Leisure Suit Larry* (1987), and *Police Quest* (1987), all of which generated numerous sequels for play on a wide assortment of computers and home video consoles.

As more advanced computers and video systems became available, such pure adventure games declined in popularity. However, a hybrid adventure game involving

LucasArts president Darrell Rodriguez (centre, right) *and BioWare co-founder Ray Muzyka* (centre, left) *don costumes to announce the development of the MMOG* Star Wars: The Old Republic *in 2009. LucsArts was a leader in graphic-based adventure games throughout the 1990s.* David McNew/Getty Images

complex puzzles, Brøderbund Software's *Myst* (1993), was the best-selling PC game in the 20th century. The game and its sequels sold well on various computer and video consoles. Graphic-based adventures didn't fade from the scene entirely, however, and the developers at LucasArts virtually defined this genre throughout the 1990s. Witty dialogue, clever puzzles, and striking visuals were hallmarks of a series that included *The Secret of Monkey Island* (1990), *Sam and Max Hit the Road* (1993), *Full Throttle* (1994), and *Grim Fandango* (1998).

ACTION-ADVENTURE GAMES

The first action-adventure game, Atari, Inc.'s *Adventure* (1979), loosely based on Crowther's text-based game, was released for the Atari 2600 home video console. The game used a top-down view and allowed players to carry and use items without inputting text commands.

The popularity of the action-adventure genre got a big boost with the release of Nintendo Co., Ltd.'s *The Legend of Zelda* (1986) for the Nintendo Entertainment System (NES; 1983). The game and its sequels continue to be among Nintendo's best-selling titles for its various video consoles. Similarly, Brøderbund's *Prince of Persia* (1989) helped to popularize the action-adventure format on PCs, and sequels have been made for most video consoles. Perhaps the single most identifiable action-adventure character is Lara Croft, star of Eidos Interactive's *Tomb Raider* (1996), which was first made for the Sega Corporation's Saturn (1994) console. It and its sequels have been made for PCs and most video consoles. In addition, two films, both starring Angelina Jolie as Lara Croft, have been released: *Lara Croft: Tomb Raider* (2001) and *Lara Croft Tomb Raider: The Cradle of Life* (2003).

Action-adventure games with horror or survival elements are also popular. Early examples that have produced several sequels for multiple platforms include Infogrames Entertainment's *Alone in the Dark* (1992), Capcom Company's *Resident Evil* (1996), and Konami Corporation's *Silent Hill* (1999).

NOTABLE ADVENTURE GAMES

Some of electronic gaming's most recognizable faces have emerged from the adventure genre, which also has provided the inspiration for numerous Hollywood films. For better or for worse, few of them have matched the entertainment quality of their source material.

Prince of Persia

Prince of Persia was an electronic action-adventure game series originally developed by the American game company Brøderbund Software in 1989 for Apple Inc.'s Apple II home computer. (Brøderbund was acquired by the Learning Company [a division of Mattel, Inc., an American toy company] in 1998.) The Prince of Persia franchise was later acquired by the French game company Ubisoft Entertainment. Originally designed by the American computer programmer Jordan Mechner, the Prince of Persia franchise boasts nearly a dozen game releases for personal computers (PCs) and various video game consoles.

The original *Prince of Persia*, which had strong platform game elements, follows the Prince, a character who begins as a beggar on a quest to reach the Princess. The game's villain, Jaffar, is attempting to rule Persia by rising to power in the Sultan's absence. In particular, Jaffar plans to marry the Princess in order to become Sultan, but a side-scrolling adventure ensues when the Prince contests that plan. As

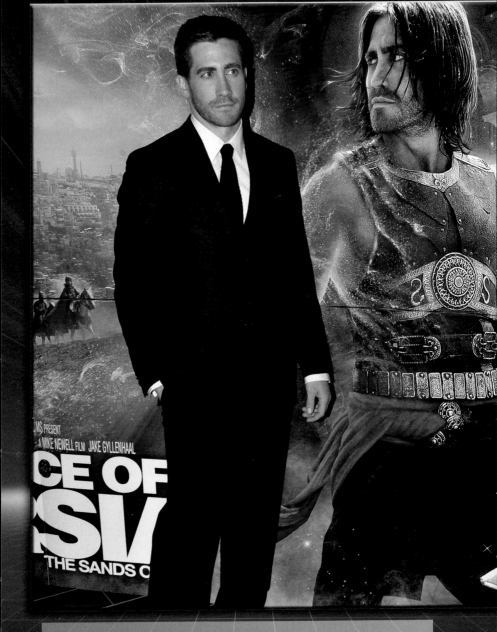

Actor Jake Gyllenhaal stands in front of a promotional poster for the 2009 movie Prince of Persia: The Sands of Time. *The film was based on Brøderbund Software's* Prince of Persia *video game.* Jon Furniss/WireImage/Getty Images

an additional challenge, the player is on a timer and has only 60 minutes to beat the game. Whenever the Prince dies, he has to restart his current level, or section of the game, and loses time. *Prince of Persia* kept players entertained with advanced graphics, challenging puzzles, and innovative twists. The original story line ended after two releases in the 1990s, but 2003 saw the release of *Prince of Persia: The Sands of Time* by Ubisoft. *The Sands of Time* was a hit, scoring high points for graphics and dynamic controls, and it ushered in two popular sequels, *The Warrior Within* (2004) and *The Two Thrones* (2005).

A graphic novel chronicling the Prince of Persia's adventures, written by Mechner, was released in 2008. Ubisoft also released *Prince of Persia* (2008) for PCs and for the Microsoft Corporation's Xbox 360 and the Sony Corporation's PlayStation 3 video game consoles. The game *Prince of Persia: Forgotten Sands* and the film *Prince of Persia: The Sands of Time* both debuted in May 2010, with Jake Gyllenhaal filling the role of the big-screen prince.

Myst

Brothers Rand and Robyn Miller designed *Myst*, a graphical puzzle-adventure electronic game, for American game manufacturers Cyan Worlds and Brøderbund Software. Debuting in 1993, its advanced graphics and an engrossing story line helped *Myst* sell fans on what was essentially a very pretty series of puzzles, which showed the industry that grenades and machine guns were not always needed to sell games. *Myst* was the best-selling computer game of all time until the gaming company Electronic Arts released *The Sims* in 2002.

In *Myst* players assume the role of the Stranger. Using magical books to travel through the island of Myst, players obtain items and complete puzzles to open up new levels, or Ages. The majority of scenarios consist of players getting clues and finding items or switches throughout the island and then using them to complete an objective. As a commercially successful software game without death, violence, hoards of enemies, or a visual barrage of noise and action, *Myst* helped pave the way for other popular titles in the same genre.

Myst spawned four direct sequels, *Riven* (1997), *Myst III: Exile* (2001), *Myst IV: Revelation* (2004), and *Myst V: End of Ages* (2005). Although the series went on to sell more than 12 million copies, the original title made up more than half the total sales, with the sequels unable to match the success of the original. The series achieved a broad cultural appeal, with English rock musician Peter Gabriel contributing his voice to *Revelation*.

Resident Evil

Capcom's savvy mix of horror, action, and puzzle-solving has made *Resident Evil* one of modern gaming's most popular and critically acclaimed series. Every release of *Resident Evil* has sold more than 1 million copies since the original's 1996 debut for the Sony Corporation's PlayStation video game console. The *Resident Evil* franchise features video games, toys, films, novels, and comic books.

The numerous incarnations of *Resident Evil* present a number of different stories, plotlines, and villains. In spite of these variations, the basics tend to remain the same: third-person perspective action dealing with hordes of mutant zombies in scary situations and settings. Raccoon City is the original and most commonly traversed area in the series. The Umbrella Corporation, a bioengineering and pharmaceutical company, operates in the background of *Resident Evil*'s stories and often is the cause of the zombies' existence. The T-Virus, which was created by Umbrella, is a contagious compound that turns everyone it infects into murderous, mutant creatures. Major releases in the *Resident Evil* franchise include *Resident Evil 2* (1998), *Resident Evil 3: Nemesis* (1999), *Resident Evil Code: Veronica X* (2001), and *Resident Evil 4* (2004). *Resident Evil 5* (2009) was a departure for the series, emphasizing action and heavy firepower over the stealth and scares of the earlier installments. It also incorporated a robust cooperative mode that made it a popular choice for online gamers.

In 2002 the first of a series of *Resident Evil* films was released. Directed by Paul Anderson and starring Milla Jovovich, the first film did not earn favourable reviews but achieved enough success to prompt a number of sequels: *Resident Evil: Apocalypse* (2004), *Resident Evil: Extinction* (2007), and *Resident Evil: Afterlife* (2010). All the films added futuristic updates to the zombie-movie genre.

Tomb Raider

The action game *Tomb Raider* was created in 1996 by British developers Core Design in partnership with Eidos Interactive Ltd. One of the most influential and critically acclaimed titles of the 1990s, *Tomb Raider* spawned many sequels and laid the groundwork for its genre with innovative graphics and fluid game play.

In the original *Tomb Raider*, players operate Lara Croft, a beautiful and voluptuous archaeologist in search of treasure. In a series of sprawling levels set in Peru, Egypt, Greece, and the lost city of Atlantis, players meet with a diverse array of challenges, ranging from shooting to dexterity and timing challenges, to puzzles. The character Jacqueline Natla, Croft's employer at the start of the game and adversary toward the end, helps round out a unique story line that was rare in platform action gaming up to that time. Croft's movement is one of the game's highlights, allowing players to sidestep, crawl, roll, dive, hang from ledges, and swim.

Tomb Raider generated more than a dozen sequels and spin-offs across virtually every gaming system and computer interface. In 2001 Angelina Jolie starred as Croft in *Lara Croft: Tomb Raider*, a film adaptation of the game. A sequel, *Lara Croft Tomb Raider: The Cradle of Life* (2003), could not match the original's success and signaled a downturn in the popularity of the game series.

Diablo

Diablo, a groundbreaking fantasy role-playing game, was released in 1997 by the American company Blizzard Entertainment (now Activision Blizzard). Set in and under the fictional city of Tristam, *Diablo* sent players on a journey through a series of dungeons to eventually do battle with Diablo, Lord of Terror. *Diablo* featured an innovative battle engine, a sprawling list of weapons, and armour and spells, and it garnered one of the first great online followings.

Diablo had two primary modes of play: single-player and multiplayer. In the solo mode, players battled it out across 16 dungeons, uncovering a deep story line and challenging enemies. *Diablo*'s multiplayer environment, one of the game's initial strengths, allowed players to compete online. Players created a character in one of three classes: Warrior, Rogue, or Sorcerer. Unlike most games in the fantasy genre, *Diablo* allowed every character to use any kind of item, spell, weapon, or armour, irrespective of class.

Diablo rose to power by virtue of Battle.net, Blizzard's free online network for playing the game. The game developed a gigantic army of fans who helped put *Diablo* on the map, but the game's online popularity also attracted legions of hackers who altered online *Diablo* games, giving impossibly powerful statistics to their characters and creating copies of extremely rare and powerful items, such as magical weapons and armour. Although the resulting lack of fair play eventually helped push *Diablo* aside, die-hard fans still advertise for games in many Internet forums. *Diablo* spawned one expansion, *Diablo: Hellfire*, and one direct sequel, *Diablo II*.

Metal Gear Solid

The Japanese toy and game company Konami released *Metal Gear Solid*, the first entry in the stealth espionage electronic game series, in 1998. The game took its inspiration from the 1980s Nintendo console classic *Metal Gear*. *Metal Gear Solid* is centred on a series of missions undertaken by retired soldier Solid Snake. In the first *Metal Gear Solid*, Snake is deployed to counteract Foxhound, a special forces unit turned terrorist. A cast of endearing characters, both good and evil, interact with Snake throughout the series and serve as the centrepiece for the game's popularity. *Metal Gear Solid* has several sequels, prequels, a novel, multiple spin-offs, a radio drama, and a series of comic books. *Metal Gear Solid* is viewed as one of the all-time best games for the Sony Corporation's PlayStation console.

The *Metal Gear Solid* series focuses on stealth and strategy. Players use a variety of techniques and tools to sneak up on and neutralize enemies, with open combat coming only as a last resort. Firearms and other weaponry are used mainly against the "bosses" at the end of each level, with a great deal of strategy also required for their defeat. Smart game play, developed characters, outstanding voice actors, and a well-written script made *Metal Gear Solid* the premier stealth action title of its time and set the standard for the genre.

The *Metal Gear* series includes *Metal Gear Solid 2: Sons of Liberty*, *Metal Gear Solid 3: Snake Eater*, *Metal Gear Solid: Portable Ops*, and *Metal Gear Solid 4: Guns of the Patriots*. In 2008 *Metal Gear Solid Mobile* was released for use on cellular telephones.

God of War

The electronic action-adventure game *God of War* was released by the Sony Corporation in 2005. Viewed by many as one of the all-time great titles for Sony's PlayStation 2 video game console, *God of War* attracted players and impressed critics with stunning visuals, a strong story, and exciting game play.

The producer and director of God of War *accept the Overall Game of the Year Award at the 2006 Interactive Achievement Awards ceremony. The game proved to be popular with players and critics. Ethan Miller/*

In *God of War*, players control Kratos, a Spartan warrior who is sent by the Greek gods to kill Ares, the god of war. As the story progresses, Kratos is revealed to be Ares' former servant, who had been tricked into killing his own family and is haunted by terrible nightmares. Armed with the Blades of Chaos, a weapon made out of two daggers attached to chains, Kratos rumbles through ancient Athens and other locations on a murderous quest to terminate the rogue god. Action in *God of War* is viewed from the third person, and advanced movements such as running, jumping, climbing, and swimming are similar to those in the *Tomb Raider* series, another adventure-game series with strong platform-game characteristics. Some of Kratos's foes can be killed only by combinations of magic and physical attacks, making combat more reliant on skill. Greek mythology powers the story, so players encounter a myriad of Minotaurs and Hydras.

God of War's popularity prompted the development of a number of direct sequels and several spin-offs. *God of War II* (2007) for the PlayStation 2 also earned favourable critical response and generated excellent sales, and *God of War III* (2010) concluded the story of Kratos's revenge in spectacular fashion.

Assassin's Creed

French game developer Ubisoft Entertainment created and distributed *Assassin's Creed* for the computer and consoles in 2007. It was one of the premier titles in the third-person stealth genre, and it was championed for its stunning visuals and original story line.

In *Assassin's Creed*, players take the role of modern-day bartender Desmond Miles, who has been captured and forced to test a machine that allows people to relive their ancestors' memories through their own DNA. Miles journeys back to 1191 and takes the role of a Crusades-era Muslim Assassin who does battle with the Knights Templar and uncovers the mystery of sacred artifacts and ancient organizations. The story is periodically interrupted by modern-day interludes as Miles deals with the side effects of the memories.

Play in *Assassin's Creed* is centred on avoiding confrontation rather than seeking it out. A meter tracks a character's visibility and the environment status as play progresses; character commands allow a player to blend in with crowds, keeping a low profile to avoid detection. Eagle vision, a unique ability, allows players to see allies and enemies in different colours, making it easier to avoid harm and to find friends. *Assassin's Creed* was a surprise hit for Ubisoft, achieving both commercial and critical success. A prequel, *Assassin's Creed: Altair's Chronicles,* was released in 2008, and *Assassin's Creed 2* reached stores in 2009.

CHAPTER 6

ELECTRONIC PLATFORM GAMES AND MUSIC GAMES

E lectronic platform games and music games are family-friendly and have wide appeal to those who would prefer to avoid the violence and mature themes found in some genres. Additionally, music games lend themselves to social gatherings, where they foster a sense of friendly competition to see who can best emulate a given performance.

THE PLATFORM GAME GENRE

The electronic platform game genre was characterized by maneuvering a character from platform to platform by jumping, climbing, and swinging in order to reach some final destination. The first genuine platform game was Nintendo Company Ltd.'s *Donkey Kong* (1981), an arcade game in which Jumpman climbed up and down ladders and jumped from platform to platform while eluding a giant ape (Donkey Kong) on his way to rescuing a woman. Jumpman, now renamed Mario and joined by his brother Luigi, returned as the star of *Mario Bros.* (1983), a two-player cooperative arcade game that was subsequently released for the Nintendo Entertainment System (NES; 1983) home video console. A vastly improved version for the NES, *Super Mario Bros.* (1985), sold more than 40 million copies, making it the best-selling video game of all time according to the *Guinness Book of World Records*. It also was the first video game to be made into a movie, *Super*

A screen shot from the Super Mario World *video game. Before becoming the star of his own game, Mario was a character known as Jumpman in the prototypical platform game* Donkey Kong. James Keyser/Time & Life Pictures/Getty Images

Mario Bros. (1993) starring Bob Hoskins, John Leguizamo, and Dennis Hopper.

By the time the next generation of 16-bit video consoles arrived, particularly the Sega Genesis (1988) and the Super Nintendo Entertainment System (SNES; 1990), platform games were essential for the success of any new system. Nintendo continued with its official mascot, Mario, in *Super Mario World* (1990). Sega had less success with platform games before *Sonic the Hedgehog* (1991), which featured the company's new mascot, a hedgehog with "attitude" that helped to establish the console with a slightly older audience.

Platform games, with their typical two-dimensional play, declined in their overall popularity as more powerful 32-bit consoles such as the Sega Saturn (1994), Sony Corporation's PlayStation (1994), and the Nintendo 64 (1995) made three-dimensional games possible. Nevertheless, they continue to be popular among younger players, and some new three-dimensional platform games have been released. Examples include *Super Mario Galaxy* (2007) for the Nintendo Wii (2006), Sony's *LittleBigPlanet* (2008) for the PlayStation 3 (2006), and Electronic Arts' *Mirror's Edge* (2008) for the PlayStation 3 and the Xbox 360 (2005).

THE MUSIC GAME GENRE

In the music game genre, players interact with the game by trying to respond accurately to onscreen musical or visual cues. This can be done by tapping specific buttons on a game controller, singing at a specific pitch, or performing a sequence of dance moves on an interactive pad. One of the earliest successful games in this genre was Konami's *Dance Dance Revolution* (1998), which was a huge arcade hit before spreading to console systems. Players of the console hits *Guitar Hero* (2005) and *Rock Band* (2007) simulated performances with controllers that resembled real instruments, and each became a popular party game. *SingStar* (2004) reversed this path, adapting the established social activity of karaoke for the console market.

NOTABLE PLATFORM GAMES AND MUSIC GAMES

An intrepid plumber named Mario and his barrel-tossing ape nemesis have certainly evolved since their arcade debut, but the basic concept of the platform game remains much the same. Music games are in many ways analogous to sports games, in that both bridge pop culture worlds in a fashion that allows players to emulate their musical or athletic heroes.

Donkey Kong

In 1981 the Nintendo Company Ltd. released one of the most influential electronic games of all time. *Donkey Kong* spawned a popular franchise and helped revive the video game industry from the doldrums that plagued it in the early 1980s. The arcade version marked the first appearance of Donkey Kong, a rampaging ape who rolled barrels down a series of platforms, and Jumpman, better known as Mario of *Mario Bros.* fame after the introduction of the Nintendo console for home play. *Donkey Kong* spawned multiple sequels, including the critically acclaimed *Donkey Kong Country* series, and it inspired a cartoon television show.

A man plays Donkey Kong, *one of the most popular and influential electronic games ever made.* Donkey Kong *is credited with reinvigorating the flagging video game industry in the early 1980s.* Jason Kempin/FilmMagic/Getty Images

The original *Donkey Kong* featured a very simple premise. Users played as Jumpman and in each level had to save Pauline, a pink-clad female character, from the giant ape Donkey Kong. Utilizing timely jumps and ladder-climbing skills, players navigated an extensive series of levels, using hammer power-ups to destroy objects and collecting bonus items along the way for additional points. *Donkey Kong* has been consistently praised for being one of the most challenging games of its era, and it marked the debut of the platform game genre. Because of a programming glitch, the game has no official ending. The timer on the 22nd level is too short for the level to be completed, so, when time runs out, the display and the game end, adding to *Donkey Kong*'s quirky mystique.

In the *Donkey Kong Country* series on the Super Nintendo system, users play as a much friendlier Kong and his sidekick, Diddy Kong, in an adventure to retrieve stolen bananas from a reptilian enemy, King K. Rool. Nintendo's popular *Mario Kart* series also features Donkey Kong as a playable character. The documentary *The King of Kong: A Fistful of Quarters* (2007), directed by Seth Gordon, examines the quest of two men to obtain and hold on to *Donkey Kong*'s highest score.

Super Mario Bros.

The spiritual successor to *Donkey Kong, Super Mario Bros.* was created by Nintendo Company, Ltd., in 1985 for the Nintendo Entertainment System. Based on the *Mario Bros.* arcade game, *Super Mario Bros.* helped launch one of gaming's most popular franchises. It stars Mario and Luigi, two Italian plumbers who find themselves in the Mushroom Kingdom trying to rescue Princess Toadstool from the evil King Bowser. It is one of the best-selling game series, with more than 40 million copies sold.

In the original *Super Mario Bros.*, solo players pilot Mario, and an additional player can play as Luigi. The game is based on a series of side-scrolling levels, each filled with enemies ranging from mushroomlike Goombas to evil turtles known as Koopa Troopas. The levels take place in different settings, some in dungeons and some above ground, with fights against Bowser impersonators at the end of castle levels. Once the imposter is defeated, a Mushroom Kingdom resident informs Mario or Luigi that the princess is in another castle. The game is completed with the defeat of the true Bowser and the rescue of Princess Toadstool.

Super Mario Bros. helped NES become a resounding success. The game inspired more than 10 direct game sequels; a television cartoon, *The Super Mario Bros. Super Show!* (1989); and a live action film, *Super Mario Bros.* (1993).

LittleBigPlanet

LittleBigPlanet was created by the British game-development company Media Molecule and released in 2008 for the Sony Corporation's PlayStation 3 (PS3) video game console. *LittleBigPlanet* is viewed as one of the flagship titles for the PS3. The game is set apart from similar games by its customization features, which allow players to design their own characters, homes, and levels. *LittleBigPlanet* has a large online community where these user-generated works are shared.

In *LittleBigPlanet*, players control Sackboys or Sackgirls, tiny doll-like creatures stitched together from cloth and stuffing, as they run, jump, and dodge their way through a variety of whimsical landscapes, solving puzzles and exploring new environments. Characters can be customized down to the smallest detail, with the different materials used for character construction having different properties. Emotions can be programmed for the Sack characters, and a variety of outfits can be designed.

In addition to the standard predesigned levels, the game features a simple content editor that allows players to create their own levels and modifications. Using the intuitive content editor, players without any computer-programming knowledge can make elaborate environments of their own design, adding an element of creativity to the game. Players can then post their new creations online and share them with *LittleBigPlanet* gamers around the world.

SingStar

SingStar, a video game adaptation of karaoke, was developed by the Sony Corporation of Japan for its video game consoles the PlayStation 2 (in 2004) and the PlayStation 3 (in 2007). It challenged the *Guitar Hero* and *Rock Band* franchises in the music-games market. *SingStar* differed from these games in one critical way: Rather than requiring players to press buttons in a specific sequence, *SingStar* players actually sang along with songs, gaining points for vocal accuracy.

SingStar provides two different coloured microphones, which players use to sing a multitude of songs in either single-player or multiplayer format. Singers earn points for precision and have the opportunity to score additional points for hitting certain notes and consistently staying on pitch. A camera, such as Sony's PlayStation Eye, can be used to simulate a music video, putting the player into the game and on the screen, with the lyrics shown below their icon, or avatar. Players can compete against one another or perform duets. Additional songs are accessible through *SingStar*'s online archive, the SingStore. The SingStore has many tracks available for download, with new songs added regularly.

SingStar has released a library of different games that focus on individual genres of music. These include *SingStar Rocks!* (2006), *SingStar Anthems* (2006), *SingStar Pop Hits* (2007), *SingStar 90s* (2007), *SingStar R&B* (2007), and *SingStar Singalong with Disney* (2008). The vast majority of these were released for the PlayStation 2, with a handful on the PlayStation 3. *SingStar* has received generally positive reviews, especially in the multiplayer format. The game has enjoyed greater popularity in Australia and Europe than it has in the United States.

Guitar Hero

A popular electronic game series, *Guitar Hero* was developed and released by American companies RedOctane, Harmonix Music Systems, and Activision (now Activision Blizzard) in 2005. Utilizing a controller modeled after a guitar, *Guitar Hero* allows users to play an expansive collection of popular rock-and-roll songs by pressing buttons on their controller to match commands displayed on the screen. Scores are determined by a player's accuracy and by the level of difficulty. Upon its release, *Guitar Hero* helped to popularize the new genre of "rhythm games" (so called because players interact with the game by rhythmically responding to onscreen musical cues).

Guitar Hero was originally inspired by the lesser-known arcade game *GuitarFreaks*. *Guitar Hero II* was released in 2006, followed in 2007 by *Guitar Hero III: Legends of Rock* and *Guitar Hero Encore: Rocks the 80s*. These releases added to the franchise's musical library and included an array of controllers modeled after the famous Gibson electric guitars. *Guitar Hero: World Tour*, released in 2008, emulated the competing music game *Rock Band* by packaging a drum kit and microphone with the guitar.

Guitar Hero quickly became a cultural icon. An episode of the animated television show *South Park* was created in homage to the game's immense popularity, and *Guinness World Records* recognized the game's highest-scoring players. *Guitar Hero* surfaced in the video for the hit song "Touch My Body" by Mariah Carey, and rock group Aerosmith extended its hit library to Activision and received its own game, *Guitar Hero: Aerosmith* (2008).

This multimedia saturation represented the high-water mark for the franchise. Immediately afterward *Guitar Hero* (and console-based music simulations as a whole) began a steady decline. Sales of later titles dropped, primarily because existing players had already bought the expensive hardware needed to play the game but also because not enough new players were adopting the game to sustain its previous momentum. Two heavy metal bands, Metallica and Van Halen, headlined *Guitar Hero* expansions in 2009, but *Guitar Hero 5*, released that same year, saw disappointing sales. The latter title was criticized by the surviving members of Nirvana for its depiction of Kurt Cobain, as the game allowed players to pair the late grunge rocker's onscreen avatar with unlikely and comical music selections. *Guitar Hero 6: Warriors of Rock* was released in 2010 and posted the worst first-month sales in franchise history. By then, many fans of rhythm games had migrated to touchpad devices such as the iPhone. Citing declining revenues, Activision Blizzard ceased development of *Guitar Hero* in February 2011.

Rock Band

Rock Band was created by the American company Harmonix Music Systems and was distributed by Electronic Arts for use with the Sony Corporation's PlayStation 2 and 3 and the Microsoft Corporation's Xbox 360 in 2007, and for the

Mötley Crüe performs during a concert promoting the release of their single Saints of Los Angeles, *the first song ever released through the video game* Rock Band. *Tim Mosenfelder/Getty Images*

Nintendo Company's Wii in 2008. *Rock Band* is similar to Activision Inc.'s gaming sensation *Guitar Hero*, but instead of focusing on the guitar, *Rock Band* features a microphone and drums as well.

Rock Band allows up to four players to perform together, using a microphone for singing and three other devices to emulate a lead guitar, a bass guitar, and drums. The game's musical instrument controllers simulate the playing of popular songs, with players trying to match their button and action inputs with those shown on-screen. Each player's accuracy is scored and contributes to the overall score. The game features more than 50 basic songs, with many more available online. The game is relatively simple in presentation but has the benefit of a sprawling musical library, allowing players to download and play through an impressive amount of music. Along with *Guitar Hero*, *Rock Band* contributed to a multiplayer musical gaming boom. Although *Rock Band* features engaging solo play, it encourages gamers to form virtual bands that can play together in person or online.

The popularity of *Rock Band* caused music industry legends to take notice. Mötley Crüe became the first rock group to release a single on *Rock Band* with their 2008 song, "Saints of Los Angeles." *Rock Band* has achieved both critical and popular success. Since its release, the franchise has expanded to include *Rock Band 2* (2008) and several additional expansion packs. Among the most successful was *The Beatles: Rock Band*, in which players assumed the roles of rock's legendary foursome. It was released on Sept. 9, 2009, the same day that Apple Corps Ltd. rereleased the entire Beatles catalog in new, digitally remastered versions

CHAPTER 7

BRAIN GAMES

The broad category of "brain games" includes a variety of games that emphasize resource management, pattern recognition, or strategic planning. Although these games tend toward the cerebral, sharp eyes and quick reflexes can be useful—most notably those in the puzzle genre. In addition to the electronic management and puzzle genres, as well as artificial life gaming, brain games also include electronic adaptations of classic board games such as chess and the ancient Chinese game of strategy, Go.

THE ELECTRONIC MANAGEMENT GAME GENRE

Management games, in which players run a business or an enterprise, did not get their start in the arcades. With its characteristic requirement for slow meticulous planning, the genre first appeared for early home computers. One of the earliest examples was *M.U.L.E.* (1983), an addictive multiplayer game of exploration and trading developed by Ozark Softscape and released by Electronic Arts for the Atari 800 and Commodore 64 home computers. In Maxis Software's *SimCity* (1989), the player handles the founding and growth of a city by laying out roads and utilities; setting up residential, commercial, and industrial zones; and building various civic improvements. Another example is Sid Meier's *Railroad Tycoon* (1990), in which the player lays track, builds stations, purchases train engines and cars,

Four titles in the Sims *video game franchise. Released in 1989, the initial title of the series,* SimCity, *was in the vanguard of the electronic management game genre.* © AP Images

devises passenger and cargo routes, and competes with computer-controlled train lines both directly and through a stock market.

Numerous sequels of the latter two games have been produced for PCs and home video consoles, but the magic of *M.U.L.E.* has eluded attempts at replication. Other early games in this genre for video consoles, such as the Nintendo Entertainment System (NES) and the Sega Genesis, include Koei Company, Limited's *Aerobiz* (1992) and Electronic Arts' *Theme Park* (1994). Another popular title was Hasbro Interactive's *RollerCoaster Tycoon* (1999) for PCs and the Microsoft Corporation's Xbox console. Peter Molyneux's *The Movies* (2005) gave Hollywood the tycoon treatment with a graphically rich simulation that allowed players to control every aspect of the movie-making process.

THE ELECTRONIC PUZZLE GAME GENRE

In the puzzle game genre, players typically use logic, pattern recognition, or deduction to resolve mental challenges. Most popular puzzle games were made for personal computers, though some of them have been adapted for play on portable gaming systems and mobile telephones. Important games in this genre include *Sokoban* (1982), *Tetris* (1985), Windows *Minesweeper* (1990), and *Lumines* (2004).

Puzzles are frequently included in other electronic game genres, such as electronic adventure games, electronic platform games, and electronic role-playing games (RPGs). For example, Brøderbund Software's *Myst* (1993), originally released for Apple Inc.'s Mac OS, is an adventure game in which the plot is driven forward as the player gathers clues to solve a series of puzzles. Media Molecule's *LittleBigPlanet* (2008), released for Sony Corporation's PlayStation 3, is a platform game that features puzzle levels created by other players.

THE ELECTRONIC ARTIFICIAL LIFE GAME GENRE

Players nurture or control artificial life (A-life) forms in the artificial life game genre. This genre was one of the first to emerge in the early days of electronic gaming. One of the earliest examples is *The Game of Life*, a cellular automaton created by the English mathematician John Conway in the 1960s. Following a few simple rules, various "organisms" evolve on the basis of where starting "seeds" are placed.

More than any other individual, American computer programmer and cofounder of Maxis Software William (Will) Wright is associated with the development of

William Wright, the cofounder of Maxis Software and the creator of the Sims *franchise.* AFP/Getty Images

commercial A-life games. His first commercial A-life release was *SimEarth* (1990), a world-builder simulation for personal computers (PCs) in which players select from various landforms and climates for their planet, seed the planet with very primitive life forms, and wait to see if advanced life will develop. Compared with his hit electronic management game *SimCity* (1989), it was a flop. Undeterred, Maxis tried again with a simpler simulation, *SimAnt* (1991), in which players take the role of a black ant (yellow in the game) as it helps its colony compete for resources with a computer-controlled colony of red ants.

Maxis followed that with the critically acclaimed *SimLife* (1992), an A-life simulation in which players adjust numerous environmental and genetic parameters to influence the evolution of plants and animals within the game. It has often been used as a tool for teaching children how plants, herbivores, and carnivores interact to maintain a sustainable ecosystem. Maxis returned to the format of *SimLife* with *Spore*, another single-player A-life game. *Spore* has several notable features. Players can upload their designed or evolved creatures to a central database that may be used to populate the A-life universe, or metaverse. Also, after evolving space-faring species, players can visit other players' home worlds. Statistics are available concerning how each player is faring compared with other players and how their creatures have interacted with other players' creations within the metaverse. Finally, players can capture video of their creatures for uploading to YouTube.

Maxis also developed *The Sims* (2000), an A-life simulation that is the best-selling game of all time for PCs. In the game players take control of one or more virtual people (Sims) and may direct virtually every aspect of their lives. *The Sims* and its sequels *The Sims 2* (2004) and *The Sims 3* (2009), which are essentially elaborate electronic dollhouses, were the first electronic games to appeal to large numbers of females.

DEEP BLUE

Deep Blue was a computer chess-playing system designed by IBM in the early 1990s. As the successor to Chiptest and Deep Thought, earlier purpose-built chess computers, Deep Blue was designed to succeed where all others had failed. In 1996 it made history by defeating Russian grandmaster Garry Kasparov in one of their six games—the first time a computer had won a game against a world champion under tournament conditions. In the 1997 rematch, Deep Blue won the deciding sixth game in only 19 moves; its 3.5–2.5 victory (it won two games and had three draws) marked the first time a current world champion had lost a match to a computer under tournament conditions. In its final configuration, the IBM RS6000/SP computer used 256 processors working in tandem, with an ability to evaluate 200 million chess positions per second.

NOTABLE BRAIN GAMES

Classical board games, tycoon games, and "god" games of every stripe comprise the broad category of brain games. This genre features some of the best work from legendary creators such as Sid Meier, Will Wright, and Peter Molyneux.

Chessmaster

Chessmaster, a popular series of computer chess games, was originally released in 1986 by the Software Toolworks, which was later acquired by the Learning Company. *Chessmaster* featured extremely competitive artificial intelligence engines—with later versions named "the King"—that challenged all but the most skilled of players and helped bring the game to virtually every make of computer and gaming system over the years. Featuring 2D and 3D game play, later versions applied technology from other popular chess games to make *Chessmaster* a universal favourite.

Early versions of *Chessmaster* were released for nearly every type of personal computer, including Amiga, Apple II, Atari 8-bit, Atari ST, ZX Spectrum, Commodore 64, Macintosh, and DOS-based machines. *Chessmaster 4000* saw the first incarnation of the King, which allowed players to create chess "personalities." These personalities, which a player would assign to his opponent, could be adjusted down to the smallest detail. By placing certain emphasis on a particular aspect of the game, such as king protection or aggressiveness, players were able to compete in a variety of game types and improve their own personal chess abilities. Personalities could be adjusted to mirror actual players, such as the former world chess champions Bobby Fischer or Mikhail Botvinnik. In 2002 *Chessmaster 9000* even won a game against the reigning U.S. chess champion, Larry Christiansen.

Railroad Tycoon

American game guru Sid Meier designed *Railroad Tycoon* for publisher MicroProse Software. This railroad management simulation game debuted in 1990 and helped launch the successful "tycoon" subgenre. The game was praised for its unique premise, which combined attributes of *SimCity* with a healthy love for all things locomotive.

In the original *Railroad Tycoon*, players were given the opportunity to run a virtual railroad, down to the smallest detail. Laying tracks, establishing stations, and rescheduling various shipments were just some of the tasks players undertook as they attempted to transform start-up money into a railroad empire. *Tycoon* differed from *SimCity* and some of the other games in the simulation genre in that there was a time limit and an element of competition. Opposing tycoons could try to put a player's fledgling railroad out of business—for example, by making stock deals and adjusting fees in an attempt to thwart a player's success—which added a realistic twist to the game.

Railroad Tycoon generated a series of spin-offs and sequels, including *Railroad Tycoon Deluxe* (1993), *Railroad Tycoon II* (1998), *Railroad Tycoon 3* (2003), and *Sid Meier's Railroads!* (2006). Although all the titles appealed to their niche, the series was plagued by software bugs and programming issues that detracted from the gaming experience. *Railroads!* was the first title since the original to have Meier as a producer, but it was criticized for lacking some of the economic features—e.g., issuing stocks and bonds, purchasing shares in other player's railroads, investing in industry—that players had come to love in the previous releases.

SimCity

SimCity was designed and produced in 1989 by American game designer Will Wright and electronic game developer Maxis (now a division of Electronic Arts). This city creation and management simulation game is viewed as a quite original game, and it spawned an array of sequels, including the very successful series *The Sims*.

Inspired by his reading and by the map-building functions of other games, Wright originally called the game *Micropolis*. Because the first incarnation of the game did not have a final ending or a winning condition, many companies did not consider it marketable, and Wright had trouble finding a software company to develop his idea. He eventually teamed up with Maxis, and *SimCity* was released to critical praise in 1989. *SimCity* allows players either to start from scratch by making their own city with funds on a blank map or to solve the problems of managing real-life cities such as Boston and San Francisco. In the game, power plants are needed to provide electricity for commercial, residential, and industrial zones, and roads have to be built to connect all areas of the city. Most aspects of city government are controllable, from taxes to ordinances on gambling and smoking. Crime, traffic congestion, and even Godzilla are a few of the challenges that players face.

Several *SimCity* sequels were generated, as well as a plethora of spin-offs including *SimAnt* (1991), *SimIsle* (1995), and *SimCopter* (1998). In *Streets of SimCity* (1997) players can drive a vehicle through the various cities built on *SimCity*, as well as through replicas of actual cities.

The Sims

Will Wright took the municipal management of *SimCity* to a more personal level with the life-simulator game, *The Sims*. It was published and distributed by the American companies Maxis and Electronic Arts in February 2000. *The Sims* was tremendously popular the first two years after its debut, selling more than six million copies. Since then a bevy of expansion packs and sequels have been produced.

In *The Sims*, players have the ability to control the lives of ordinary people. Players orchestrate the mundane daily activities of characters, including the intricate workings of the virtual dating world; the degree to which these activities are successful is contingent on the soundness of the players' decisions. *The Sims* provides a world of nearly infinite freedom, allowing players to determine the type and quality of life for their characters. As a character, or "Sim," progresses, new elements are integrated into the game. Sufficiently advanced Sims acquire additional family members, find better jobs, and inhabit nicer homes, which the players themselves design. In general, the game features a highly sophisticated architectural system and artificial-intelligence engine for the characters.

As with the immensely popular *SimCity* gaming franchise, *The Sims* has its own language—a combination of Ukrainian and Tagalog known as "Simlish"—and its own culture. The fan base for *The Sims* is unique in that a large percentage of the community consists of female players, a rarity in the video game world.

Spore

Having simulated city management and the daily activities of virtual humans, Wright's next creation allowed players to control the basic elements of life itself. *Spore* was released by Electronic Arts in 2008 for Microsoft Corporation's Windows OS and Apple Inc.'s Mac OS.

A scene from the electronic artificial life game Spore. *Players compete as various species that develop and gain skills as their creators complete tasks*

Spore lets players create a species from the most basic elements, starting out with a single-celled organism.

Spore combines real-time strategy with the total control characteristic of the "god game" genre to produce a unique and extremely deep gaming experience. With what the game calls "Creatiolutionism," players customize and develop their species from the ground up, with a goal of eventually traveling through space and overtaking an advanced species called the Grox. As players complete missions and phases, their unique race develops and acquires skills.

Spore is a single-player game, though it is based online and has a community that is supported by the video-sharing Web site YouTube (owned by the search-engine company Google, Inc.). Players can upload videos of their work to *Spore*'s YouTube channel; the best videos earn badges for the players, which can be used to upgrade equipment in the game. *Spore* also features Sporecast, an RSS feed that allows players to keep track of their favourite creators and creations. *Spore* received positive reviews from most gaming magazines and Web sites for its creativity and scope, with the primary criticisms being a lack of depth in the early stages and a level of play that was more appealing for casual players than veteran gamers. An expansion pack, *Spore Creepy & Cute Parts Pack* (2008), provided an array of new additions to the game.

CHAPTER 8

ELECTRONIC ROLE-PLAYING GAMES

Like their pen-and-paper counterparts, players of electronic role-playing games advance through a story quest, and often many side quests, for which their character or party of characters gain experience that improves various attributes and abilities. The genre is almost entirely rooted in TSR, Inc.'s *Dungeons & Dragons* (*D&D*; 1974), a role-playing game (RPG) for small groups in which each player takes some role, such as a healer, warrior, or wizard, to help his party battle evil as directed by the group's Dungeon Master, or assigned storyteller. While fantasy settings remain popular, electronic RPGs also have explored the realms of science fiction and the cloak-and-dagger world of espionage.

SINGLE-PLAYER RPGS

Early electronic RPG games generally kept some or all of the original aspects of *D&D*, including its fantasy world of elves, dwarfs, trolls, goblins, and dragons and its character attributes—constitution, strength, dexterity, intelligence, wisdom, and charisma. The first effort to produce an electronic version of *D&D* was *Dungeon* (1975), which was an unauthorized adaptation for the Digital Equipment Corporation PDP-10 minicomputer. Although basically a text-based implementation, it included overhead maps of the dungeon that showed where players had explored.

The first commercial *D&D*-style games were Origin Systems, Inc.'s *Ultima* (1980) and Sir-Tech Software, Inc.'s *Wizardry* (1981), both originally for Apple Inc.'s Apple II home computer. Sequels of *Wizardry* were produced over the next two decades for the Commodore Amiga computer, personal computers running MS-DOS, and the Sega Saturn and Sony Corporation PlayStation home video consoles. Similarly, sequels of *Ultima* (now owned by Electronic Arts) were made over the next 25 years for the Amiga, Apple's Mac OS, Microsoft Corporation's Windows OS, and video game consoles from Nintendo, Sega, and Sony.

Popular single-player RPG franchises for home video consoles include Square Enix's *Dragon Quest* (1986–) and *Final Fantasy* (1987–), for Nintendo and Sony consoles, and Sega's *Phantasy Star* (1987–), for Sega and Sony consoles. Nintendo's *Pokémon* (1995–) series is the most successful RPG franchise in terms of total media sales (games, cards, books, figurines), and the most recent versions include support for playing against others over the Internet.

Traditionally, computer gamers had been treated to a deeper gameplay experience, with richer, more complex stories than those found on early consoles. A standout example of this was *Ultima IV: Quest for the Avatar* (1985), in which players' characters were directly affected by the ethical choices they made. By the 1990s, however, console games had made great strides, with titles like Square Enix's *Chrono Trigger* (1995) and *Final Fantasy VII* (1997) redefining gamers' expectations. Soon, outstanding games such as Eidos Interactive's *Deus Ex* (2000) and BioWare Corporation's *Star Wars: Knights of the Old Republic* (2003) were winning fans on both PCs and consoles. Other popular RPGs for Windows OS, Mac OS, and next generation consoles include BioWare's *Baldur's*

Dozens of Pokémon action figures line the shelves at the 2009 Tokyo Toy Show. Figurines and video games are just two of the components of the immensely successful role-playing franchise. Junko Kimura/Getty Images

Gate (1998–), *Mass Effect* (2007–), and *Dragon Age* (2009–) franchises; and Bethesda Softworks' *Fallout* (1997–) and *The Elder Scrolls* (1994–) series.

MULTIPLAYER RPGS

Persistent multiplayer game worlds, known as massively multiplayer online role-playing games (MMORPGs), have their origin in early text-based multiuser dungeons played on mainframe computers and minicomputers. Because the introduction of graphics in RPGs pushed early PCs and telephone connection speeds to their limits, most of the first graphical multiplayer RPGs settled for small worlds limited to a few players. For example, AOL's *Neverwinter Nights* (1991–97) at first limited the game world to a few dozen players on its proprietary dial-up network. Similarly, Blizzard Entertainment's *Diablo* (1997), an action-oriented game with some RPG elements, which was originally released for Windows OS and later for the Mac OS, included the ability for four players to enter the game's world together by signing up through the company's Battle.net game hosting service.

The most popular early MMORPGs for Windows OS were Electronic Arts' *Ultima Online* (1997–) and Sony's *EverQuest I & II* (1999–). Though still persisting, the number of subscribers to these games declined significantly as MMORPGs with improved graphics were released. Sony also runs the game server for Square Enix's *Final Fantasy XI* (2002–), also known as *Final Fantasy XI Online*, for the PlayStation 2, Windows OS, and Microsoft's Xbox 360; its large user base is concentrated in Japan, where it is highly popular.

The leaders in the "second generation" of MMORPGs include Blizzard's *World of Warcraft* (2004–) for Windows OS and Mac OS, Turbine, Inc.'s *Lord of the Rings Online* (2007–) for Windows OS, and Electronic Art's *Warhammer Online* (2008–) for Windows OS. *World of Warcraft* became so popular that it created an employment category, known as "gold farmer," in China, where thousands of players accumulate game resources to sell through the global online auction and trading company eBay.

NOTABLE ELECTRONIC ROLE-PLAYING GAMES

Immersing oneself in the complex story of a single-player RPG campaign or joining thousands of others in the ongoing narrative of a shared online world can provide some of the most rewarding experiences in electronic gaming. The memorable characters and events of well-executed role-playing games can leave impressions as rich and lasting as those of any book or film.

Final Fantasy

Final Fantasy was created in January 1987 by Japanese game manufacturer SquareSoft (now Square Enix, Inc.). The first installment of the long-running role-playing game (RPG) series was playable on the Nintendo Entertainment System. The game spawned numerous sequels on a variety of platforms, ranging from Nintendo's console to the Sony PlayStation series, Microsoft's Xbox, and Windows OS-based PCs.

Final Fantasy is strongly rooted in the fantasy tradition, and the game includes many magical and fantastical elements. The game and its successors also embrace the world of technology, and, consequently, the distinctive *Final Fantasy* universe has frequently been situated within the corresponding "steampunk" genre. In general, there is a recognizable cast of core characters or character types, such as mages (magicians) and knights, each with unique abilities. These abilities, along with an assortment of weapons and items, are used in the characteristic menu- and turn-based combat system throughout the game. As the hero and his accompanying party defeat enemies, they gain experience points and "gil" (the game world's currency), allowing them to gain new powers and buy better equipment.

One of the most important elements of *Final Fantasy* is the narrative. The complex plot that governs the game play is representative of the entire franchise: it focuses on good and evil, and the hero must surmount a range of obstacles to defeat the primary villain. In subsequent games in the series, the plot and character development became increasingly intricate and central to the gaming experience.

A crowd gathers at a Tokyo store waiting to purchase the latest installment in the Final Fantasy *video game franchise, 2009.* AFP/Getty Images

From its start as a Nintendo game available only in Japan, the series grew into an international phenomenon with a significant fan following and a robust community on the Internet. *Final Fantasy's* place in the annals of video game history has been secured by its status as a classic among RPG enthusiasts and by the sheer number of its sequels, which run into double digits.

Pokémon

Nintendo debuted *Pokémon* in Japan in 1995, and it later became a global phenomenon. The series, originally produced for the company's Game Boy console, was introduced to the United States in 1998 with two titles, *Red* and *Blue*. In the games, players assume the role of

RICHARD GARRIOTT

Richard Garriott, a British-born American computer-game developer, was born on July 4, 1961, in Cambridge, Eng. He grew up in Houston, the son of National Aeronautics and Space Administration (NASA) astronaut Owen Garriott, who first flew into space on July 28, 1973, as part of the Skylab 3 mission. Many of the Garriotts' friends and neighbours were astronauts, and Garriott developed an early interest in spaceflight.

While Garriott never abandoned his dreams of spaceflight, his interests and career path took him into the computer-gaming industry. As a teenager, Garriott began working on a fantasy role-playing game called *Akalabeth* (1979) for the Apple II. In the 1980s, while attending the University of Texas at Austin, he expanded on the dungeon-crawling model of *Akalabeth* to create *Ultima 1*. The *Ultima* series that followed established him as a major player in the computer-gaming industry, and in 1983 Garriott cofounded Origin Systems, Inc. Garriott's in-game avatar, Lord British, ruled the kingdom of Britannia, and players engaged in quests to defeat a series of evils.

With the debut of *Ultima IV: Quest of the Avatar* (1985), players were faced with ethical dilemmas as well as challenges of might and magic. Non-player characters (NPCs) could converse more realistically, and Britannia was now a fully realized world, with shifting winds and a predictable lunar cycle. In 1997 Garriott and his team created *Ultima Online*, a pioneer in the burgeoning genre of online computer games. Three years later he started Destination Games, which later became part of NCsoft, the world's largest online-game developer and publisher. In November 2007 he launched the multiplayer online computer game *Tabula Rasa*.

Garriott became the sixth space tourist when, after training at the Yury Gagarin Cosmonaut Training Centre in Star City, Russia, he launched aboard Soyuz TMA-13 on Oct. 12, 2008, with commander Yury Lonchakov of Russia and flight engineer Edward Fincke of the United States. He arrived at the International Space Station (ISS) two days later. Garriott's work on the ISS included communicating with students via radio signals, taking photographs for the Nature Conservancy, and conducting experiments on the physiological effects of space travel. He landed in Kazakhstan aboard Soyuz TM-12 on Oct. 23, 2008. His trip was made possible by Space Adventures, Ltd.—an American company that made space travel available to high-paying clients—in which Garriott was an investor.

Pokémon trainers, obtaining cartoon monsters and developing them to battle other Pokémon. Pokémon became one of the most successful video game franchises in the world, second only to Nintendo's Super Mario Bros.

The original *Pokémon* is a role-playing game based around building a small team of monsters to battle other monsters in a quest to become the best. Pokémon are divided into types, such as water and fire, each with different strengths. Battles between them can be likened to the simple hand game rock-paper-scissors. For example, to gain an advantage over a Pokémon that cannot beat an opponent's Charizard character because of a weakness to fire, a player might substitute a water-based Pokémon. With experience, Pokémon grow stronger, gaining new abilities. By defeating Gym Leaders and obtaining Gym Badges, trainers garner acclaim.

Pikachu, a yellow mouse, is the undisputed face of Pokémon and helped the series become a worldwide phenomenon. Pokémon inspired a cartoon series, movies, books, a toy line, sequels, spin-offs, a clothing line, and a popular trading-card game. In spite of a friendly interface and little violence, Pokémon has not been without controversy. In 1999 the parents of two nine-year-old boys sued Nintendo, stating that the Pokémon card game had caused the children to develop gambling problems and likening the trading-card craze to an illegal lottery. Religious groups that discount the theory of evolution have also targeted Pokémon for showing Pokémon evolving into new creatures.

Fallout

American game developer Interplay Entertainment released the first entry in the RPG *Fallout* franchise in

1997 for personal computers (PCs). *Fallout* contained many traditional RPG elements, such as turn-based play and characters that evolve as experience is gained, but it added a variety of innovations that earned the title much critical acclaim.

In the first *Fallout* game, set in a postapocalyptic world in the year 2161, the player's character resides in a fallout shelter known as Vault 13. When a device that recycles water for the shelter's residents breaks, the character must venture into a barren landscape to find a replacement part. The mission turns into a quest to stop an evil mutant called "The Master" from unleashing a virus that will turn all human beings into mutants. Other wasteland-dwelling human characters can be recruited to aid the character in foiling the mutant takeover. The

A game character stands guard on the red carpet during the 2008 Los Angeles launch of Interplay Entertainment's Fallout 3. John Shearer/WireImage/ Getty Images

game is viewed from above and features a version of California that has been wrecked by nuclear devastation. *Fallout* includes a "karma" rating that is affected by the decisions made in the game, such as whether a player chooses to help various game characters in side quests or more strictly pursue the main quest. The story and the ending of the game are influenced by how players conduct their characters.

Fallout featured well-known voice-acting talent such as Ron Perlman, Tony Shalhoub, and Brad Garrett. Sequels *Fallout 2* (1998), for PCs, and *Fallout 3* (2008), the first in the series to also be released for console systems, were also well received, cementing the franchise's status as a classic in the RPG genre. *Fallout* has appeared on the all-time best games lists of a number of prominent gaming magazines and Web sites.

Baldur's Gate

Baldur's Gate, an influential computer and console RPG, was developed by Canadian company BioWare Corp. and released in 1998 by the American game publisher Interplay Entertainment Corporation. *Baldur's Gate* is set in the Forgotten Realms fantasy universe of the popular *Dungeons & Dragons* franchise. Generating numerous spin-offs and expansions, *Baldur's Gate* was viewed as a comeback for the lagging role-playing game genre in the late 1990s.

Primary game play for the original *Baldur's Gate* depicted an overhead view of an environment. Plot and story devices were developed through dialog and events in battle, as players developed and improved their own characters, or avatars. As with most games in the genre, the player's avatar and travel companions earn experience points as they progress through the game, allowing them to gain new abilities and strengths. *Baldur's Gate* features seven chapters and a story line that uncovers the heritage and dark family ties of a player's character, with twists and turns along the way.

Baldur's Gate received favourable reviews upon its release, and it was named 1998 Game of the Year by a number of industry leaders. A series of novels based on *Baldur's Gate* was produced; die-hard fans of the game, however, have protested differences in story and character trends. The sequel *Baldur's Gate II: Shadows of Amn* (2000) expanded on the success of the original with additional character classes, a branching story line that provided hundreds of hours of gameplay, and subplots based on characters' moral choices and romantic interests that greatly added to the game's replay value.

Kingdom Hearts

An RPG released by Japanese game manufacturer SquareSoft (now Square Enix, Inc.) for the PlayStation 2 in 2002, *Kingdom Hearts* joined two popular fantasy universes: the cartoon world of the Disney Company and the world of SquareSoft's *Final Fantasy* video game franchise. *Kingdom Hearts* saw great success, enjoying strong sales and critical acclaim that spawned several sequels and spin-offs.

The game features Sora, a human character similar to others from the *Final Fantasy* series, and Disney legends Donald Duck and Goofy, who together journey through the world of Kingdom Hearts. Maleficent, the evil sorceress from Disney's animated feature film *Sleeping Beauty*, bands together with other Disney villains to gain access to everyone's hearts. The majority of locations that Sora and his animated crew explore in trying to stop

Maleficent are taken directly from Disney film lore, such as the city of Agrabah from *Aladdin*. Many characters from *Final Fantasy* make cameos as well, including Cid Highwind from *Final Fantasy VII* and Rikku from *Final Fantasy X*. Many references are made throughout the game's story to both worlds, seamlessly blending the two as the player battles droves of the "heartless," the game's stock enemy type.

Kingdom Hearts was one of the best-selling PlayStation 2 titles in North America. Praised for its originality and beautiful presentation, the game sat atop many critics' "best of" lists, and it even prompted the creation of a popular manga-style graphic-novel series. A sequel, *Kingdom Hearts: Chain of Memories*, was released for the Nintendo GameBoy Advance in 2004, and a third installment, *Kingdom Hearts 2*, was released for the PlayStation 2 in 2005. The prequel *Kingdom Hearts: Birth by Sleep* (2010) was released exclusively for Sony's hand-held PSP system.

CHAPTER 9

ELECTRONIC FIGHTING GAMES AND VEHICLE GAMES

I n electronic fighting games and vehicle games, players compete against computer-controlled opponents or each other in matches that test a player's speed and skill. Many fighting and vehicle games also feature specific button combinations that activate special moves or powerful combinations on an unsuspecting foe.

THE ELECTRONIC FIGHTING GAME GENRE

The electronic fighting game genre features competitive matches between a player's character and a character controlled by another player or the game. Such matches may strive for realism or include fantasy elements. The genre originated in Japanese video arcades and continues primarily on home video consoles, especially in online matches.

EIGHT-BIT ERA

The first fighting game to allow combat between two player-controlled characters was Sega Corporation's *Heavyweight Champ* (1976), a black-and-white 8-bit arcade

A Capcom employee shows the company's Street Fighter IV *game on Apple's iPhone and iPad. The original* Street Fighter *debuted on an 8-bit arcade console.* Yoshikazu Tsuno/AFP/Getty Images

console simulation in which two boxers are shown in profile, or two dimensions, with the players able to throw only high (head) or low (body) punches. The next step in the development of fighting games was Data East Corporation's *Karate Champ* (1984), an arcade console that had a limited repertoire of punches and kicks.

Konami's *Yie Ar Kung-Fu* (1985) added a variety of punch and kick maneuvers, each activated by moving the joystick in a specific direction—an innovation that would be greatly expanded by later games—as well as a "health bar" that indicated a player's relative strength. Capcom's *Street Fighter* (1987) also introduced a more elaborate set of special moves. However, all of these 8-bit arcade consoles suffered from underpowered computer chips and poor control sticks that made it difficult to execute the precise sequences needed for special combat moves.

Sixteen-Bit Era

The real breakthrough for this genre occurred with the introduction of Capcom's 16-bit arcade game *Street Fighter II* (1991), which had vastly improved hardware that supported better graphics and special button-pushing combinations to perform elaborate combat moves. Another popular 16-bit fighter was Midway Manufacturing Company's *Mortal Kombat* (1995), which used digitized images of real people and large quantities of realistic looking blood and gore. Both of these games developed a cult following and spawned film versions: *Street Fighter* (1994), starring Jean-Claude Van Damme, and *Mortal Kombat* (1995), starring Christopher Lambert.

Three-Dimensional Fighting Games

Although the first three-dimensional fighting game, Mindscape, Inc.'s *4D Sports Boxing* (1991), was actually released for various early personal computers, it had little impact on the development of the fighting genre. This honour goes to Sega's arcade console *Virtua Fighter* (1993). *Virtua Fighter* was noteworthy for its realistic depiction of combat, with various playable characters that specialized in different schools of martial arts. Although Namco Limited's *Tekken* (1994–) came later, it has lasted through numerous sequels and been ported to most home video consoles. Another long-lasting series is Tecmo, Inc.'s *Dead or Alive* (1996–), which is noteworthy for its introduction of a system of countermoves (and counters to counters, ad infinitum).

Together with electronic vehicle games, especially auto racing, these fighting games revitalized arcades in the 1990s. In particular, millions of players spent untold hours honing their skills against one another for local bragging rights. Such contests eventually led to regional, national, and international competitions.

Home Console Games

Two reasons for the decline of arcades in the 1990s were the steep learning curve for newcomers to the fighting games and the increasing power of home video consoles. As the 16-bit home consoles, such as the Sega Genesis (1988) and the Super Nintendo Entertainment System (SNES; 1990), arrived on the market, gamers found that they could play fighting games at home with graphics that rivaled those found in the arcades. And with the arrival of the 32-bit home consoles, such as the Sega Saturn (1994), Sony Corporation's PlayStation (1994), and the Nintendo 64 (1995), it was the home console games that began setting the graphic standards for the fighting genre. Among the most important early home fighting games was *Tekken 2* (1995), an arcade game that was ported to the PlayStation in 1996.

While the graphics were improving for home systems, many players missed the competitive atmosphere found in arcades. Their concerns were addressed with the release of 64-bit consoles, such as the Sega Dreamcast (1998), PlayStation 2 (2000), and the Microsoft Corporation's Xbox (2001). In particular, the Dreamcast included a modem for connecting players over the Internet, Microsoft launched Xbox Live (2001), an Internet-based subscription gaming service, and Sony responded in 2002 with a modem for the PlayStation 2.

Two boys challenge each other to an electronic wrestling match using the Xbox 360, at a 2011 IT show in Singapore. Roslan Rahman/AFP/Getty Images

The next generation of video consoles, the Xbox 360 (2005) and PlayStation 3 (2006), featured still greater integration of proprietary gaming networks and consoles. Although many of the most popular fighting games, such as *Tekken* and *Mortal Kombat*, are available in versions for both platforms, players cannot compete across these networks.

THE ELECTRONIC VEHICLE GAME GENRE

As the name implies, the electronic vehicle game genre involves players controlling an assortment of vehicles. Typically players engage in races or in combat against vehicles controlled by other players or the game itself.

RACING GAMES

Pole Position (1982), created by Namco Limited of Japan and released in the United States by Atari Inc., was the first racing game to become a hit in arcades. The single-player game featured Formula 1 racing cars, 8-bit colour graphics, the race course used at Japan's Fuji Speedway, and competition with several computer-controlled cars. The game has been ported to various home video game systems, as well as Apple Inc.'s iPhone. In 1987 Namco and Atari released *Final Lap*, a multiplayer sequel that ran on several 16-bit computer chips from Motorola, Inc.

Still greater adherence to realistic driving was achieved with the arrival of 32-bit arcade machines. Among the more popular of these newer games were *Virtua Racing* (1992), from the Sega Corporation of Japan, and Namco's *Ridge Racer* (1993).

From the very beginning, auto racing games, often ported from early arcade consoles, were popular on 8-bit home video systems such as the Nintendo Entertainment System (NES; 1983) and the Sega Master System (1985). With the launch of 16-bit home consoles, such as the Sega Genesis (1988) and the Super Nintendo Entertainment System (SNES; 1990), some long-lasting racing series were introduced. In particular, Nintendo's Mario Kart series was launched with *Super Mario Kart* (1992), a go-kart racing game that has been upgraded in sequels for each of the company's subsequent consoles.

The arrival of 32-bit home systems, such as the Sega Saturn (1994) and the Sony Corporation's PlayStation (1994), signaled the first real challenge to the arcades for preeminence in racing games. Among the most successful—and realistic—series are Electronic Arts's *Need for Speed* (1994–), which has been produced for all the major 32-bit and subsequent consoles, and Sony's *Grand Turismo* (1997–) for the PlayStation, PlayStation 2 (2000), and PlayStation 3 (2006) consoles.

In addition to straight racing games, car games with combat components have been around since Bally Midway's *Spy Hunter* (1983), an arcade game in which the player chases and shoots at a spy while trying not to run over or shoot civilians on the roads. An example of an electronic adventure game with prominent automobile sequences is Rockstar Games's multi-platform series *Grand Theft Auto* (1997–), in which players often steal cars and try to elude police.

COMBAT GAMES

One of the earliest combat vehicle games was Atari's *Tank* (1974), a black-and-white arcade game for two people in which the players each used two joysticks to maneuver their tanks around an obstacle-strewn field while shooting at each other. Atari also produced two of the earliest arcade combat flight games—*Pursuit* (1975), a single-player simulation of World War I dogfights, and *Jet Fighter* (1975), a two-player game with more modern aircraft.

Combat vehicle games for personal computers and home video consoles almost always deliberately simplify the controls, though not always as much as arcade versions, in order to make them playable without lengthy training. One groundbreaking console title was *B-17 Bomber* for Mattel's Intellivision system. Players crewed a B-17 Flying Fortress on bombing missions over Europe, switching between roles as navigator, bomber, pilot, and gunner, as voices generated by a speech synthesizer alerted them to incoming fighters, flak, or an approaching target. Several popular aerial combat games have been based on movies.

The best-known films adapted for game play include *Top Gun* (1986), released the following year as a licensed game by different companies for several types of home computers and the NES console, and *Flight of the Intruder* (1991), released by Mindscape in the same year as a licensed game for the NES.

With the arrival of the Internet, several multiplayer aerial combat games developed a following. Popular titles include HiTech Creation's *Aces High* (2000) for PCs; Ubisoft's *IL-2 Sturmovik* (2001) and *Blazing Angels* (2006) for PCs, Microsoft Corporation's Xbox, the PlayStation 3, and Nintendo's Wii; and Incognito Entertainment's *Warhawk* (2007) for the PlayStation 3.

In addition to games based on real military vehicles, several games are based on players controlling or donning advanced machines from the world of science fiction. One of the most influential series is *MechWarrior* (1989–), based on the board game *BattleTech* (1984), now owned by Topps, Inc. In addition to arcade versions, *MechWarrior* has been produced by different companies for PCs and home video consoles from Nintendo, Sega, Sony, and Microsoft. *TIE Fighter* (1994), a space combat simulator from LucasArts, put players at the controls of one of the most recognizable ships in the Star Wars universe. The game's precise controls, realistic flight mechanics, and engaging story line have led to its inclusion on many critics' lists of the best games of all time.

NOTABLE ELECTRONIC FIGHTING GAMES AND VEHICLE GAMES

Flying fists and squealing tires are hallmarks of electronic fighting games and vehicle games. The titles below inspire some of the most spirited player-on-player competition in electronic gaming.

Street Fighter

The electronic fighting game series *Street Fighter* was originally released as an arcade game in 1987 by the Japanese game manufacturer Capcom. The popular arcade game gave rise to an entire genre of fighting games and spawned a multitude of sequels and spin-offs.

The first *Street Fighter* was a side-scrolling kick-and-punch game, similar to *Double Dragon* or *Final Fight*. The main player controlled Ryu, and a second player could join in by controlling Ken; together they fight their way through challengers using martial arts moves. With the release of the groundbreaking *Street Fighter II: The World Warrior* in 1991, the formula shifted to player-versus-player round-based combat. Players selected characters from a roster of fighters with unique styles from around the world. Special moves were available by keying in directional pad and button combinations, which added an extra level of skill to the game.

Staying relevant throughout multiple generations of gaming, *Street Fighter* helped pave the way for such games as *Mortal Kombat*, *Soulcalibur*, and *Killer Instinct*. Although *Street Fighter* was originally produced as an arcade game, many titles in the series have been released for a variety of gaming platforms, including video game consoles and personal computer systems. In 1994 *Street Fighter* was made into a live-action film directed by Steven Souza and starring Jean-Claude Van Damme. Although critically panned, the movie showcased many of *Street Fighter*'s popular characters. A second movie based on the series, titled *Street Fighter: The Legend of Chun-Li,* was released in 2009.

Mortal Kombat

Mortal Kombat was a video game series created by the Midway Manufacturing Company of the United States.

KOLLECTOR'S EDITION NT

Bonus
Inclu
See Bac
Detai

MORTAL KOMBAT®
DECEPTION™

MATURE 17+

M

CONTENT RATED BY
ESRB

Game Experience May
Change During Online Play

MIDWAY®

High levels of blood and graphic violence precipitated a "Mature Audiences
Only" rating—indicated by the "M" in the lower left corner of the game
package—for Mortal Kombat. Business Wire/Getty Images

Mortal Kombat debuted as a two-dimensional arcade game in 1992 and went on to become one of the most popular video games in the 1990s. The original arcade game spawned many sequels and expansions across a wide array of console gaming systems, generated a line of toys, and inspired two motion pictures: *Mortal Kombat* (1995) and *Mortal Kombat: Annihilation* (1997).

In *Mortal Kombat* players select one of many unique characters to battle against other fighters in a gauntlet-style tournament to determine who faces the final "boss." Among the game's notable points is a vast catalogue of special techniques for each fighter that can be performed by entering an intricate series of commands on the controller. One of these techniques, the *finishing move*, gained particular notoriety because, if players quickly pressed the right combination of buttons on the controller, the defeated opponent would be brutally maimed, humiliated, or otherwise defiled.

REGULATION

The level of blood and gore in the 16-bit arcade games and the emerging home console versions—including depictions of hearts being plucked out of chests and heads, along with their attached spines, being ripped out of bodies—led to political pressure for censorship, or at least parental warnings, in many communities around the world. In the United States, Sen. Joseph Lieberman led congressional investigations (1992–93) into video game violence and its purported effects on society. In response several organizations were created by industry leaders to establish a rating system. The Entertainment Software Rating Board's advisory code for video and computer games was formally approved by the U.S. Congress in 1994. The code has been revised several times, both in terms of categories and in wording, though critics contend that code designations remain too arbitrary, with games containing similar levels of sex and violence often getting quite different ratings.

Because of the excessive amount of simulated blood, violence, and gore, *Mortal Kombat* faced intense public scrutiny. In fact, *Mortal Kombat* and other comparable games eventually gave rise to the Entertainment Software Rating Board. The advent of a rating system resulted in later versions of the game featuring the ability to restrict the violence in the game via game-play settings, but, as the series was founded on characters spraying blood and falling into spiked pits, the game's premise and overall feel remained the same. As advances in technology and a departure from *Mortal Kombat*'s classic style began, the game faded in popularity and sales.

Grand Theft Auto

American company Rockstar Games developed *Grand Theft Auto*, and it was published in 1997 and 1998 by the American Softworks Corporation (ASC Games) for play on video game consoles and personal computers. After an immensely popular debut, *Grand Theft Auto* went on to generate multiple sequels and expansions, including *Grand Theft Auto: Vice City* (2002), *Grand Theft Auto: San Andreas* (2004), and the critically lauded *Grand Theft Auto IV* (2008).

In the *Grand Theft Auto* series, gamers control criminals and attempt to increase their standing by completing missions in various virtual cities. The first game of the series offered a simple bird's-eye perspective of the landscape from which the gamer could view and engage in carjacking, robberies, gun fights, and other forms of delinquency. Approaching a vehicle and removing the driver allows the player to take control of the vehicle, change the radio stations, and wreak as much havoc as necessary to complete the objectives. Later games in the series offered improved graphics and different modes of play. Strategically placed video clips develop the story line, giving each title its own distinct narrative and characters. The ability to move about the cities freely—combined with intricate and challenging levels—made *Grand Theft Auto* one of the most innovative and popular gaming titles of the late 1990s.

David Jones, the designer of *Grand Theft Auto*, also designed the successful *Lemmings* video game series in 1991, and his decision to help create the long-running *Grand Theft Auto* series proved financially wise, considering its tremendous popularity among many gamers. *Grand Theft Auto*'s unique style and appealing game play helped convince celebrities such as singer Phil Collins and actors Burt Reynolds and Samuel L. Jackson to provide voice cameos for the game.

CHAPTER 10

ELECTRONIC STRATEGY GAMES

The electronic strategy games genre emphasizes strategic or tactical planning, involving the control of multiple units rather than the quick reflexes typical of electronic shooter games. There are two major types of electronic strategy games: turn-based strategy (TBS) and real-time strategy (RTS). Although some TBS games have experimented with multiplayer support, the slow pace of waiting for each player to finish managing all of his or her resources and units has limited their appeal. On the other hand, players expect modern RTS games to include support for, or be focused entirely on, multiplayer contests.

TURN-BASED GAMES

Electronic strategy games are rooted in board games, particularly war games, or strategic simulations of war. Thus, one of the first successful electronic strategy games was *Eastern Front (1941)*, a turn-based re-creation of Germany's World War II invasion of Russia that was released for the Atari video game console in 1981. Although numerous TBS games have come and gone for personal computers, a few franchises continue to release new versions that dominate the genre. A particularly long-lasting series is Koei Company, Ltd.'s *Romance of the*

A poster promotes the animated series Romance of the Three Kingdoms *in China, 2009. A video game featuring the same theme and characters has been popular in China and Japan for decades.* © AP Images

Three Kingdoms (1985–), based on the Chinese novel of the same name, which features political and historical themes rooted in China during the 2nd and 3rd centuries CE, when the land was divided between three large kingdoms (Shu, Wei, and Wu). The Japanese company has also released versions in the series for several generations of home video consoles.

Another long-lasting franchise is Sid Meier's *Civilization* (1991–), an American series that has set the standard for TBS games in which the player takes a tribe and nurtures it through centuries of progress from the stone age to the space age. A simplified, quicker-playing version with online multiplayer support, *Civilization Revolution* (2008), was released for Sony Corporation's PlayStation 3. Strategy met high fantasy in the *Heroes of Might and Magic* series (1995–) from New World Computing, and *X-COM: UFO Defense* (1993) by Culture Brain is regarded as one of the finest science fiction TBS games ever released. An example in the genre that abandoned almost all strategic elements for tactical play is SquareSoft's *Final Fantasy Tactics* (1997) for the PlayStation, which combined elements from *Final Fantasy* (1987–), an electronic role-playing game series, with turn-based unit tactics.

REAL-TIME GAMES

As personal computers became more powerful, real-time games became viable, with the first commercial success being *Dune II* (1992), based on American director David Lynch's 1984 film version of Frank Herbert's science fiction novel *Dune* (1965). *Dune II* allowed players to select and control multiple units with their mouse for the first time, creating the control interface standard for most subsequent RTS games, such as Blizzard Entertainment's *Warcraft* (1994–), Westwood Studios' *Command & Conquer* (1995–), and Microsoft Corporation's *Age of Empires* (1997–).

Bungie Software's *Myth* (1997) and *Myth II* (1998), which focused exclusively on tactical play, were noteworthy for their inclusion of editing tools that enabled players to modify various aspects of the games, including complete mods ("modifications") that turned the fantasy-based warfare into reenactments of battles in the American Civil War or World War II. In 2000 Bungie was acquired by the Microsoft Corporation, and while the company continued to support Bungie.net, a free online gaming network, Bungie soon turned its resources to developing the electronic first-person shooter (FPS) game *Halo*. When Bungie.net closed in 2002, fans of the games reverse-engineered the server software and set up new servers, which continued to support network play of the original games and the mods until 2007.

NOTABLE ELECTRONIC STRATEGY GAMES

Whether turn-based or real-time, strategy games can easily consume many hours, with players telling themselves that they'll quit "after this turn" or "as soon as I beat this level." Although computer AI responses have greatly improved over time, the greatest challenges can be found in head-to-head matches against human opponents.

Romance of the Three Kingdoms

A statistics-based strategy game series launched in 1985 by Japanese electronic game developer Koei Co., Ltd., *Romance of the Three Kingdoms* features turn-based play, along with many unique features that set it apart from other war and conquest games. With releases across virtually every gaming medium, *Romance* is highly popular in Japan, South Korea, and the United States. It has political and historical themes rooted in China during the 2nd and 3rd centuries CE, when the land was divided between three large kingdoms (Shu, Wei, and Wu).

    Romance is based on managing various statistics related to the cities and characters in the game. As the ruler of a Chinese kingdom, a player improves the kingdom's statistics to effectively do battle with other kingdoms located on a historical map of China. Everything from loyalty to food storage to battle skills is weighed in the game, which requires patience and strategy. In *Romance*'s first release, players could assume only one role, but later releases offered the option of playing as an adviser, a prefect, a general, or a vassal. The time frame and political themes in the series are based on the 14th-century historical novel *Romance of the Three Kingdoms* (*Sanguozhi yanyi*), traditionally ascribed to Luo Guanzhong.

Romance of the Three Kingdoms, with more than a dozen sequels, has been praised for the exceptional scope that it offers for skillful play, especially in multiplayer games.

Civilization

Sid Meier created *Civilization*, a popular TBS franchise. The first installment was published by his U.S.-based MicroProse computer software company in 1991.

Meier had experience creating flight simulator games prior to his work in the "God game" genre, where players have total control over multiple facets of the game. Meier created *Railroad Tycoon* first and built upon the success of its more involved gameplay, expanding on the format in *Civilization*. In this latter game, which involves a single player competing against the game software, the player first selects a civilization and then develops it, while sharing the virtual world and its resources with a number of computer-controlled civilizations. Players can control diplomatic relations and trade with other civilizations, oversee the economy of their own civilizations, and use their military forces aggressively or as a deterrent. There are a number of ways to win the game, including militarily, through diplomacy, or with a space-race victory.

Subsequent related games have created one of the most successful series in computer gaming history. Sequels to the game or add-on packs to a specific version of the game have improved the game's graphics; given the player more choices of leaders, civilizations, and in-game units; and expanded upon the number of ways to win the game and interact with competitors. Fan sites and official forums provide a venue for amateur "modders" to modify the game's units and scenarios and to share modifications with other players to further enhance the quality, variety, and performance of the game. *Civilization* set the standard for all subsequent strategy-based games and "God games," two overlapping genres that comprised the most popular style of video game in the early 2000s.

Command & Conquer

American game developer Westwood Studios launched *Command & Conquer*, a real-time strategy (RTS) series in 1995. Initially using the engaging *Dune II* (1992) as its model, the groundbreaking *Command & Conquer* franchise has produced a number of primary spin-offs and sequels, setting a new standard for longevity and consistency in a gaming series.

The original release in the series, *Command & Conquer: Tiberian Dawn*, pitted the Global Defense Initiative of the United Nations against the rogue Brotherhood of Nod. Both factions were after Tiberium, an otherworldly resource that sucked up nutrients in the ground and formed large crystals that could be harvested. Players gathered Tiberium crystals to build various structures, allowing them to produce different types of soldiers and war vehicles. Using the terrain, unit matchups, and formations, opposing armies fought in a variety of scenarios. The game allowed a single player to progress through a series of missions or multiple players to wage war together online.

Rich Hilleman of Electronic Arts accepts the Strategy/Simulation Game of the Year Award bestowed upon Command and Conquer 3: Tiberium Wars *at the 2007 Interactive Achievement Awards.* Ethan Miller/Getty Images

Command & Conquer's universe is vast, and the franchise has spread across many battlefields, realities, eras, and planets since its inception. Later releases in the series include the prequel *Command & Conquer: Red Alert* (1996), which portrayed a parallel world in which Adolf Hitler never came to power and the Soviet Union and the Allied forces battled for control of Europe. *Command & Conquer: Red Alert 3* (2008) depicted an alternate reality in which World War II had never occurred and a powerful Soviet Union battled the Allied forces and the Empire of the Rising Sun for supremacy. *Command & Conquer 4*

(2010) was billed as the conclusion to the story that was introduced in the first game, but its gameplay differed radically from previous entries in the franchise, discarding the "gather resources, build, attack" formula in favour of a fluid battlescape that emphasized map control over resource production.

Age of Empires

The *Age of Empires* computer game franchise was designed by Ensemble Studios, an American company founded in 1995 and subsequently acquired by the Microsoft Corporation. The original *Age of Empires* debuted in 1997 to critical acclaim and helped set the bar for the real-time strategy game genre, combining involved play and technical innovations with historical accuracy. *Age of Empires* generated a number of spin-offs, expansions, and sequels, including *Age of Empires II: The Age of Kings* and *Age of Mythology*.

Age of Empires allowed players to wage war against opponents in realistic settings in a real-time environment. As with tabletop war games, *Age* players commanded their armies from the "sky," directing pieces across a board, or map. All the *Age* titles provided an extensive list of civilizations, such as Roman or Aztec, to start with, each with its own strengths and weaknesses. Using villager units, players could develop the entire economy of a nation or simply get enough food to feed an army as they advanced their charges through time, measured in ages. As the characters became more advanced, they developed better technology that made them more formidable in battle. *Age of Empires* offered a sophisticated multiplayer and online play option, as well as a series of historical campaigns that involved challenging scenarios.

During the rise of real-time strategy, many players became frustrated with the game-controlled opponents of other similar titles. Instead of allowing the game's artificial intelligence to bend the game's rules, the creators of *Age of Empires* took great pride in offering a game in which the computer opponent had to win with better strategies and improved resource management rather than with unfair advantages.

StarCraft

Developed and published by Blizzard Entertainment (now a division of Activision Blizzard) and released in March 1998, *StarCraft* went on to become one of the most successful real-time strategy (RTS) games of all time.

Gamers play the online version of StarCraft II *at the 2011 CeBIT IT fair in Germany. Leagues have formed to play this popular and enduring multiplayer game.* Johannes Eisele/AFP/Getty Images

StarCraft incorporated many of the features that were regarded as standard for the RTS genre (it built on many of the conventions previously used by Blizzard in the *Warcraft* game franchise), but it integrated those elements in a way that set it apart from its contemporaries. In the game's solo campaign, the player assumed control of each of the game's three races: the human Terrans, the technologically advanced Protoss, and the insectoid Zerg. Unlike many RTS games, wherein the opposing sides generally offered a distinct visual appearance but a virtually identical play experience, the races of *StarCraft* required radically different playing styles. Zerg tactics relied on cheap, plentiful units designed to swarm an opponent, while Protoss armies consisted of a comparatively small number of expensive, powerful units. Terrans struck a balance between the two, with units that were modestly priced and relatively plentiful.

As engaging as the single-player campaign was, *StarCraft's* enduring popularity was largely a result of its robust multiplayer mode. Online play was facilitated by Battle.net, Blizzard's free game-hosting and matchmaking platform, and nowhere was *StarCraft's* multiplayer success more obvious or lasting than in South Korea. When *StarCraft* was released, high-speed Internet access was rapidly expanding in South Korea, and young people would frequently gather at a PC *bang* ("computer room") to socialize and play online games. As one of the most popular multiplayer games at the time, *StarCraft* became a national phenomenon, spawning numerous professional leagues and prompting the creation of television networks dedicated to electronic gaming. In the decade following its release, more than 10 million copies of the game sold worldwide, and of these it was estimated that approximately one-half of them had been sold in South Korea. Although its graphics and interface looked dated compared with later RTS titles, *StarCraft* remained an immensely popular multiplayer game more than a decade after its release.

BLIZZARD ENTERTAINMENT

Blizzard Entertainment, an American developer and manufacturer of electronic games, was best known for the *Diablo*, *Warcraft*, and *StarCraft* franchises and for the massively multiplayer role-playing game *World of Warcraft*.

Blizzard Entertainment was founded in 1991 as Silicon & Synapse by Allen Adham, Michael Morhaime, and Frank Pearce, three UCLA graduates with an interest in electronic gaming. The company's early projects were conversions of existing titles for a variety of home computer systems, but it soon released a number of original titles, including *The Lost Vikings* (1992), a clever platform game, and *Rock 'N' Roll Racing* (1993), a vehicle combat game. The company changed its name to Blizzard Entertainment in 1994, shortly before it released *Warcraft: Orcs & Humans*, a real-time strategy game (RTS) that became one of the definitive works in that genre. Blizzard followed with *Warcraft 2: Tides of Darkness* (1995), a graphically rich expansion on the original that offered a number of interface and multiplayer improvements.

Multiplayer would figure heavily in Blizzard's future success. The action role-playing game *Diablo* (1996) launched with Battle.net, a free service that allowed players to join multiplayer games and chat online. Battlenet's player base expanded dramatically with the release of *StarCraft* (1998), an RTS game loosely based on the *Warcraft* model. Although *StarCraft* featured an engaging single-player campaign, its true strength was in its well-balanced multiplayer mode.

The best-selling *Diablo II* (2000) refined the multiplayer elements that made the first *Diablo* a success. *Warcraft 3: Reign of Chaos* (2002) incorporated limited role-playing elements into the standard RTS formula, and it allowed end users to create new game maps, import new sound effects, and radically alter the gameplay experience.

The next entry in the *Warcraft* franchise deviated dramatically from the RTS roots of its predecessors, but it provided Blizzard with its biggest hit to date. *World of Warcraft* (*WoW*), a massively multiplayer online role-playing game, debuted in 2004, and it drew millions of players to the shared, persistent online world of Azeroth. The game built on the mythology of the earlier *Warcraft* titles, with orcs, dwarves, elves, and other fantasy tropes featuring prominently, but the social networking aspects of the game were perhaps its greatest strengths. In October 2010, almost six years after *WoW*'s release, the game boasted more than 12 million monthly subscribers.

In 2008 Blizzard's parent company, Vivendi Games, merged with Activision, an entertainment software publisher that traced its roots to the original Atari game console. At the conclusion of the merger, in which Activision was the senior partner, Vivendi purchased 52 percent of the stock in the newly formed Activision Blizzard. Both Activision and Blizzard maintained distinct corporate identities, with independent development and publishing streams. Blizzard's first major post-merger release, *StarCraft II: Wings of Liberty*, reached stores in July 2010, accompanied by an upgraded version of Battle.net. The matchmaking platform was redesigned to more closely resemble online content distributors such as Valve Corporation's Steam client or Apple's iTunes service, as well as to provide a smoother transition between the single player and multiplayer experience.

Brood War, an official expansion pack that featured additional single-player content and dozens of new multiplayer maps, was released in November 1998, and a console version of *StarCraft* was unveiled for the Nintendo 64 system in June 2000. After years of anticipation, *StarCraft II: Wings of Liberty* debuted in July 2010. It retained the core elements of *StarCraft* and continued the single-player story where the original had left off. It also featured vastly improved graphics and customizable game elements, similar to those found in role-playing games, that allowed players to upgrade or modify individual classes of units.

Disgaea

Disgaea, an RPG and strategy hybrid, was released by the Japanese video game company Nippon Ichi Software for the Sony Corporation's PlayStation 2 console in 2003 under the title *Netherworld Battle Chronicle: Disgaea*. It was released in the United States the same year under the title *Disgaea: The Hour of Darkness*. The award-winning game prompted multiple spin-offs and sequels.

The plot centres on Prince Laharl, a demon who resides in Netherworld, a kingdom once ruled by his father. When Laharl wakes up from a two-year nap to discover his father is dead, he sets out to claim Netherworld as his own. Along the way, Laharl joins a sprawling cast of unique and colourful characters, whose humorous interactions are one of the game's true strengths. In a departure from typical role-playing games (RPGs), *Disgaea*'s primary mode is a sequence of set battles that take place on grid-based maps with various features in each square of the grid. Game play is similar to that of genre defining turn-based tactics games such as *Final Fantasy Tactics* and *Ogre Battle*. Players develop and fine-tune a small party of warriors who face off against a similar party of enemies. Victory is obtained when one side wipes out the other. A vast number of weapons, techniques, and advances are available in the game—the pursuit of which can, for some players, overshadow or even replace the main quest.

Later releases in the series include *Disgaea 2: Cursed Memories* (2006) for the PlayStation 2 and *Disgaea 3: Absence of Justice* (2008) for the PlayStation 3, as well as a number of spin-offs. New downloadable characters for use in *Disgaea 3* have been made available over Sony's PlayStation Network (PSN). *Disgaea*'s board-game style also made it a good fit for portable gaming devices, such as the Sony PSP and the Nintendo DS, for which versions of the series have been produced.

Myth

American electronic game manufacturer Bungie Software debuted the real-time tactical combat game series *Myth* in 1997. Dropped into a market already glutted with the legendary *Warcraft* and *Command and Conquer* series, *Myth* set itself apart by focusing on warfare tactics and ignoring economic and resource development, offering a purer battle-based experience.

In *Myth* players control groups of units, including human swordsmen, elven archers, Molotov cocktail-throwing dwarves, and journeymen (healers). Play is heavily dependent on knowing how to take advantage of the units' different abilities, with swordsmen able to quickly close in on and butcher archers, archers able to shoot down frail dwarves from a safe distance, and dwarves able to blow up swordsmen before they can be reached. In single-player games, players must use their battalions to accomplish various goals in a quest-style game. In multiplayer action, players first choose units, with different associated "costs," for their armies, and then warfare begins on predetermined maps customized for one of many different battle types. These types include everything from capture the flag to a hunting game in which players compete to see who can kill the most animals.

One factor that sets *Myth* apart from other games in the genre is its dedicated fan base. *Myth* fans have provided extensive volunteer programming and updating to keep the series fresh and enjoyable for other die-hard fans. *Myth* spawned two direct sequels, *Myth II: Soulblighter* (1998) and *Myth III: The Wolf Age* (2001).

CONCLUSION

Having evolved from its humble beginnings in university computer labs to a thriving multibillion-dollar global enterprise, electronic games have come to occupy a flourishing pop culture niche. Family-friendly options, such as the Nintendo Wii, open the door to inexperienced gamers, while titles such as *God of War* and the *Grand Theft Auto* franchise continue to revolutionize gameplay for a mature audience. Whether using a mobile gaming device as a diversion during a long commute or delving into the character-driven world of the latest RPG release, engaging in a fierce Pokémon battle or joining other virtual warriors for an online first-person shooter match, generations of gamers have established electronic gaming as a way to occupy the leisure hours of people of every age.

APPENDIX: NOTABLE ELECTRONIC GAMES

SHOOTER GAMES

Year	Title	Developer
1962	*Spacewar!*	Digital Equipment Corporation
1971	*Computer Space*	Nutting Associates
1978	*Space Invaders*	Taito Corporation
1979	*Asteroids*	Atari Inc.
1980	*Missile Command*	Atari Inc.
1992	*Wolfenstein 3-D*	id Software
1993	*Doom*	id Software
1996	*Duke Nukem 3D*	3D Realms
1996	*Quake*	id Software
1997	*GoldenEye 007*	Rareware
1998	*Half-Life*	Valve Corporation
1999	*Unreal Tournament*	Epic Games and Digital Extremes
2001	*Halo*	Microsoft Corporation
2002	*Battlefield: 1942*	Electronic Arts
2003	*Counter-Strike*	Valve Corporation
2003	*Call of Duty*	Infinity Ward
2004	*Halo 2*	Microsoft Corporation

Year	Title	Developer
2004	*GoldenEye: Rogue Agent*	Electronic Arts
2007	*Half-Life 2*	Valve Corporation
2007	*Halo 3*	Microsoft Corporation
2007	*Team Fortress 2*	Valve Corporation
2007	*Crysis*	Crytek Studios
2007	*Bioshock*	2K Boston
2008	*Left 4 Dead*	Valve Corporation
2009	*Call of Duty: Modern Warfare 2*	Infinity Ward
2010	*Bioshock 2*	2K Marin

SPORTS GAMES

Year	Title	Developer
1972	*Pong*	Atari Inc.
1987	*Punch-Out!*	Nintendo Company
1988	*John Madden Football*	Electronic Arts
1990	*PGA Tour*	Electronic Arts
1991	*NHL*	Electronic Arts
1993	*FIFA*	Electronic Arts
1993	*Bill Walsh College Football*	Electronic Arts
1994	*NBA Line*	Electronic Arts
1996	*Triple Play*	Electronic Arts

Year	Title	Developer
1997	*NFL Blitz*	Midway Games
1998	*Knockout Kings*	Electronic Arts
1999	*NBA 2K*	Visual Concepts
1999	*Tony Hawk's Pro Skater*	multiple
2001	*Pro Evolution Soccer*	Konami Corporation
2001	*WWF Smackdown!*	Yuke's Company
2004	*Madden NFL 2005*	Electronic Arts
2006	*Wii Sports*	Nintendo Company
2006	*Major League Baseball 2K6*	2K Sports
2008	*NHL 09*	EA Canada
2009	*UFC 2009 Undisputed*	Yuke's Media Creations

ADVENTURE GAMES

Year	Title	Developer
1975	*Adventure*	Will Crowther
1977	*Zork*	Infocom
1979	*Adventure*	Atari, Inc.
1984	*King's Quest*	Sierra Entertainment
1986	*Space Quest*	Sierra Entertainment
1986	*The Legend of Zelda*	Nintendo Company

Year	Title	Developer
1987	*Leisure Suit Larry*	Sierra Entertainment
1987	*Police Quest*	Sierra Entertainment
1989	*Prince of Persia*	Brøderbund Software
1992	*Alone in the Dark*	Infogrames Entertainment
1993	*Myst*	Brøderbund Software
1996	*Resident Evil*	Capcom Company
1996	*Tomb Raider*	Eidos Interactive
1997	*Diablo*	Blizzard Entertainment
1998	*Metal Gear Solid*	Konami Corporation
1999	*Silent Hill*	Konami Corporation
2000	*Diablo II*	Blizzard Entertainment
2003	*Prince of Persia: The Sands of Time*	Ubisoft Entertainment
2003	*Silent Hill 3*	Konami Corporation
2005	*God of War*	Sony Corporation
2007	*Assassin's Creed*	Ubisoft Entertainment
2008	*Tomb Raider: Underworld*	Crystal Dynamics

Year	Title	Developer
2008	*Prince of Persia*	Ubisoft Entertainment
2008	*Silent Hill: Homecoming*	Konami Corporation
2010	*Heavy Rain*	Quantic Dream

PLATFORM GAMES

Year	Title	Developer
1981	*Donkey Kong*	Nintendo Company
1983	*Mario Bros.*	Nintendo Company
1985	*Super Mario Bros.*	Nintendo Company
1990	*Commander Keen*	id Software
1990	*Super Mario World*	Nintendo Company
1991	*Sonic the Hedgehog*	Sega Corporation
1994	*Earthworm Jim*	Shiny Entertainment
1996	*Crash Bandicoot*	Naughty Dog
1996	*Super Mario 64*	Nintendo Company
1997	*Castlevania: Symphony of the Night*	Konami Corporation
2001	*Jax and Daxter*	Naughty Dog

Year	Title	Developer
2002	*Ratchet & Clank*	Insomniac Games
2005	*Psychonauts*	Double Fine Productions
2007	*Super Mario Galaxy*	Nintendo Company
2008	*LittleBigPlanet*	Sony Corporation
2008	*Mirror's Edge*	Electronic Arts
2009	*New Super Mario Bros. Wii*	Nintendo Company
2010	*Mega Man X*	Capcom

MANAGEMENT GAMES

Year	Title	Developer
1989	*SimCity*	Maxis Software
1990	*Railroad Tycoon*	Sid Meier (MicroProse)
1992	*Aerobiz*	Koei Company
1994	*Theme Park*	Electronic Arts
1999	*RollerCoaster Tycoon*	Hasbro Interactive
2003	*SimCity 4*	Maxis Software
2004	*RollerCoaster Tycoon 3*	Hasbro Interactive
2005	*The Movies*	Lionhead Studios
2006	*Railroads!*	Sid Meier (Firaxis Games)
2009	*Tropico 3*	Haemimont Games

PUZZLE GAMES

Year	Title	Developer
1982	*Sokoban*	Hiroyuki Imabayashi
1983	*Bomberman*	Hudson Soft
1985	*Tetris*	Alexey Pajitnov
1989	*Klax*	Atari Inc.
1990	*Loopz*	Mindscape
1990	*Windows Minesweeper*	Microsoft Corporation
1991	*Lemmings*	DMA Design
1993	*Lemmings 2: The Tribes*	DMA Design
2000	*Lemmings Revolution*	Take-Two Interactive
2001	*Bejeweled*	PopCap Games
2004	*Lumines*	Q Entertainment
2005	*Crazy Machines*	FAKT Software
2006	*Lumines II*	Q Entertainment
2007	*Portal*	Valve Corporation
2008	*Elefunk*	Sony Corporation
2009	*Scribblenauts*	5th Cell

ARTIFICIAL LIFE GAMES

Year	Title	Developer
1990	*SimEarth*	Maxis Software
1991	*SimAnt*	Maxis Software
1991	*Jones in the Fast Lane*	Sierra Entertainment
1992	*SimLife*	Maxis Software
1996	*Harvest Moon*	Victor Interactive Software
2000	*The Sims*	Maxis Software
2002	*The Sims Online*	Maxis Software
2002	*Animal Crossing*	Nintendo Company
2003	*Second Life*	Linden Lab
2004	*The Sims 2*	Maxis Software
2008	*Spore*	Maxis Software
2008	*Animal Crossing: City Folk*	Nintendo Company
2009	*The Sims 3*	Maxis Software

ROLE-PLAYING GAMES

Year	Title	Developer
1980	*Ultima*	Origin Systems, Inc.
1981	*Wizardry*	Sir-Tech Software, Inc.
1985	*The Bard's Tale*	Interplay Entertainment

Year	Title	Developer
1987	*Final Fantasy*	Square Enix, Inc.
1987	*Phantasy Star*	Sega Corporation
1991	*Neverwinter Nights*	AOL
1995	*Pokémon*	Nintendo Company
1996	*Suikoden*	Konami
1997	*Ultima Online*	Electronic Arts
1997	*Final Fantasy VII*	Square Enix, Inc.
1997	*Fallout*	Black Isle Studios
1998	*Lineage*	NCsoft
1998	*Baldur's Gate*	BioWare Corporation
1999	*EverQuest*	Sony Corporation
2000	*Baldur's Gate II: Shadows of Amn*	BioWare Corporation
2002	*Final Fantasy XI Online*	Square Enix, Inc.
2002	*Kingdom Hearts*	Square Enix, Inc.
2003	*Disgaea*	Nippon Ichi Software
2003	*Star Wars: Knights of the Old Republic*	BioWare Corporation
2004	*World of Warcraft*	Blizzard Entertainment
2004	*Fable*	Big Blue Box Studios
2005	*Guild Wars*	ArenaNet
2006	*The Elder Scrolls IV: Oblivion*	Bethesda Softworks
2007	*Lord of the Rings Online*	Turbine, Inc.

Year	Title	Developer
2008	*Fallout 3*	Bethesda Softworks
2008	*Warhammer Online*	Electronic Arts
2009	*Dragon Age: Origin*	BioWare Corporation
2010	*Mass Effect 2*	BioWare Corporation

VEHICLE GAMES

Year	Title	Developer
1974	*Tank*	Atari Inc.
1975	*Pursuit*	Atari Inc.
1975	*Jet Fighter*	Atari Inc.
1982	*Pole Position*	Namco Limited
1983	*Spy Hunter*	Bally Midway
1986	*Top Gun*	multiple
1987	*Final Lap*	Namco Limited
1989	*MechWarrior*	Dynamix, Inc.
1990	*Secret Weapons of the Luftwaffe*	Lucasfilm Games
1991	*Flight of the Intruder*	Mindscape
1992	*Virtua Racing*	Sega Corporation
1992	*Super Mario Kart*	Nintendo Company
1993	*Ridge Racer*	Namco Limited
1994	*Need for Speed*	Electronic Arts

Year	Title	Developer
1994	*TIE Fighter*	LucasArts
1995	*Twisted Metal*	SingleTrac
1997	*Gran Turismo*	Sony Corporation
1997	*Grand Theft Auto*	Rockstar Games
1998	*Falcon 4.0*	Microprose
2000	*Aces High*	HiTech Creation
2001	*IL-2 Sturmovik*	1C
2001	*Project Gotham Racing*	Bizarre Creations
2006	*Blazing Angels*	Ubisoft Entertainment
2007	*Warhawk*	Incognito Entertainment
2009	*Forza Motorsport*	Turn 10
2010	*MotoGP 09/10*	Capcom

STRATEGY GAMES

Year	Title	Developer
1981	*Eastern Front (1941)*	Chris Crawford
1985	*Romance of the Three Kingdoms*	Koei Company
1991	*Civilization*	Sid Meier (MicroProse)
1992	*Dune II*	Westwood Studios
1994	*Warcraft*	Blizzard Entertainment
1995	*Warhammer*	Mindscape
1995	*Heroes of Might and Magic*	New World Computing

Year	Title	Developer
1995	*Command & Conquer*	Westwood Studios
1997	*Age of Empires*	Microsoft Corporation
1997	*Final Fantasy Tactics*	Square Enix, Inc.
1997	*Myth*	Bungie Software
1998	*Myth II*	Bungie Software
1998	*StarCraft*	Blizzard Entertainment
1998	*Nobunaga's Ambition*	Koei Company
2001	*Shattered Galaxy*	Kru Interactive
2002	*Heroes of Might and Magic 4*	New World Computing
2006	*Warhammer: Mark of Chaos*	Mindscape
2007	*Romance of the Three Kingdoms XI*	Koei Company
2008	*Civilization Revolution*	Sid Meier (Firaxis)
2009	*Nobunaga's Ambition: Iron Triangle*	Koei Company

GLOSSARY

artificial life A computer simulation of biological life.

avatar An electronic image that represents, and is manipulated by, a computer user or gamer.

console An electronic system that connects to a display (such as a television set) and is used primarily to play video games.

electronic role-playing game Electronic game in which players take on characters that advance through one or more quests and whose attributes and abilities are enhanced with experience.

first-person shooter (FPS) Describes a shooter game in which the player has a first-person perspective through his or her character.

FORTRAN (Formula Translation) A computer programming language that resembles algebra in its notation and is widely used for scientific applications.

guild A group of players, usually organized by rank, that participate together in online games against other groups; also called a clan.

hacker A person who illegally gains access to and sometimes tampers with information in a computer system.

interactive fiction A text-based adventure game with a narrative structure wherein the actions of the characters are controlled by the player via text prompts.

joystick A device by which gamers control the action of a video game, capable of motion in two or more directions.

LISP (list processing) A computer programming language designed for easy manipulation of data strings; used extensively for artificial intelligence work.

machinima Real-time, 3D filmmaking within a virtual environment that often employs graphics from a video game; short for "machine cinema."

massively multiplayer online game (MMOG) An electronic game supporting hundreds or thousands of players, usually in an interminable virtual universe; often available only on a subscription basis.

microprocessor Any of a type of miniature electronic device that contains the control circuitry necessary to perform the functions of a digital computer's central processing unit.

mod Short for "modification," referring to a change to an existing game—a new character, level, story line, or other feature—that can be shared or distributed among users.

non-player character (NPC) A character in an electronic game that does not represent a real-world player and is either programmed to deliver certain responses or is controlled by administrators of the game.

peer-to-peer Type of computer network in which each computer acts as both a server and a client—supplying and receiving files—with bandwidth and processing distributed among all members of the network.

photoreceptor A receptor for light stimuli.

platform The computer architecture and equipment using a particular operating system.

real-time strategy A genre of electronic strategy game in which human and computer players interact in real time.

social network An online community of individuals who exchange messages, share information, and, in some cases, cooperate on joint activities.

turn-based strategy A genre of electronic strategy game in which all players must take turns.

BIBLIOGRAPHY

Leonard Herman, *Phoenix: The Fall & Rise of Videogames*, 3rd. ed. (2001); and Van Burnham (ed.), *Supercade: A Visual History of the Videogame Age, 1971– 1984* (2001), provide descriptive and historical information about early arcade and television console games. David Sudnow, *Pilgrim in the Microworld* (1983); and Geoffrey R. Loftus and Elizabeth F. Loftus, *Mind at Play: The Psychology of Video Games* (1983), provide different insights into the psychological appeal and addictive qualities of the arcade and video games of the early 1980s.

Steven Poole, *Trigger Happy: Videogames and the Entertainment Revolution* (2000); and Mark J.P. Wolf (ed.), *The Medium of the Video Game* (2001), suggest ways to view the content and technology of computer games as the creation of a new entertainment medium. David Sheff, *Game Over: How Nintendo Conquered the World* (1993, reissued 1999); and David Kushner, *Masters of Doom: How Two Guys Created an Empire and Transformed Pop Culture* (2004) provide detailed business histories of two very different game companies and the personalities that shaped them. Nick Montfort and Ian Bogost, *Racing the Beam: The Atari Video Computer System* (2009) examines the technological and cultural impact of that console and some of its most influential games. Insights into the cultural, social, and political history of computer games, including issues around video game violence and gender, are provided by Justin Cassell and Henry Jenkins (eds.), *From Barbie to Mortal Kombat: Gender and Computer Games* (1998). The effect of video games on education is discussed in James Paul Gee, *What Video Games Have to Teach Us About Learning and Literacy* (2003). J.C. Herz, *Joystick Nation: How Videogames Ate Our Quarters, Won Our Hearts, and Rewired Our Minds* (1997); Harold Goldberg, *All Your Base Are Belong to Us: How Fifty Years of Videogames Conquered Pop Culture* (2011); and Steven L. Kent, *The Ultimate History of Video Games: From Pong to Pokémon—The Story Behind the Craze That Touched Our Lives and Changed the World* (2001), survey many of these issues, while providing personal impressions and interviews. Jesper Juul, *A Casual Revolution: Reinventing Video Games and Their Players* (2010), provides a careful discussion of casual games and their impact on the industry.

Marc Saltzman (ed.), *Game Design: Secrets of the Sages*, 4th ed. (2002), presents many topics of game design and technology through interviews with historically important designers. Tristan Donovan, *Replay: The History of Video Games* (2010) examines the history of the industry through its creators, with special attention paid to gaming developments in Europe and Australia.

INDEX